Somerville and Ross

THE IRISH WRITERS SERIES
James F. Carens, General Editor

TITLE	*AUTHOR*
SEAN O'CASEY	Bernard Benstock
J. C. MANGAN	James Kilroy
W. R. RODGERS	Darcy O'Brien
STANDISH O'GRADY	Phillip L. Marcus
PAUL VINCENT CARROLL	Paul A. Doyle
SEUMAS O'KELLY	George Brandon Saul
SHERIDAN LEFANU	Michael Begnal
AUSTIN CLARKE	John Jordan
BRIAN FRIEL	D. E. S. Maxwell
DANIEL CORKERY	George Brandon Saul
EIMAR O'DUFFY	Robert Hogan
MERVYN WALL	Robert Hogan
FRANK O'CONNOR	James Matthews
GEORGE MOORE	Janet Egleson
JAMES JOYCE	Fritz Senn
JOHN BUTLER YEATS	Douglas Archibald
LORD EDWARD DUNSANY	Zack Bowen
MARIA EDGEWORTH	James Newcomer
MARY LAVIN	Zack Bowen
OSCAR WILDE	Edward Partridge
SOMERVILLE AND ROSS	John Cronin
SUSAN L. MITCHELL	Richard M. Kain
J. M. SYNGE	Robin Skelton
KATHARINE TYNAN	Marilyn Gaddis Rose
LIAM O'FLAHERTY	James O'Brien
IRIS MURDOCH	Donna Gerstenberger
JAMES STEPHENS	Birgit Bramsback
BENEDICT KIELY	Daniel Casey
EDWARD MARTYN	Robert Christopher
BRENDAN BEHAN	John Stewart Collis
DOUGLAS HYDE	Gareth Dunleavy
EDNA O'BRIEN	Grace Eckley
CHARLES LEVER	M. S. Elliott
BRIAN MOORE	Jeanne Flood
SAMUEL BECKETT	Clive Hart
ELIZABETH BOWEN	Edwin J. Kenney
JOHN MONTAGUE	Frank Kersnowski
ROBERT MATURIN	Robert E. Lougy
GEORGE FITZMAURICE	Arthur E. McGuinness
MICHAEL MCCLAVERTY	Leo F. McNamara
FRANCIS STUART	J. H. Natterstad
PATRICK KAVANAGH	Darcy O'Brien
BRINSLEY MACNAMARA	Raymond J. Porter
AND GEORGE SHIELS	
STEPHEN MACKENNA	Roger Rosenblatt
JACK B. YEATS	Robin Skelton
WILLIAM ALLINGHAM	Alan Warner
SAMUEL LOVER	Mabel Worthington
FLANN O'BRIEN	Bernard Benstock
DENIS JOHNSTON	James F. Carens
WILLIAM LARMINIE	Richard J. Finneran

SOMERVILLE
AND ROSS

John Cronin

Lewisburg
BUCKNELL UNIVERSITY PRESS

© 1972 by Associated University Presses, Inc.

Associated University Presses, Inc.
Cranbury, New Jersey 08512

Library of Congress Cataloging in Publication Data

Cronin, John, 1928–
    Somerville and Ross.

    (The Irish writers series)
    Bibliography: p.
    1. Somerville, Edith Anna Œnone, 1858–1949.
    2. Martin, Violet Florence, 1862–1915. I. Title.
    PR6037.06Z595   823′.8′09   78-126031
    ISBN 0-8387-1167-8
    ISBN 0-8387-7698-1 (pbk.)

Printed in the United States of America

Contents

5

Acknowledgments

The author gratefully acknowledges the permission granted by Sir Patrick Coghill who is the nephew and literary heir and executor of the estate of Edith Somerville and the cousin of Violet Martin. He has kindly consented to the reprinting of the numerous extracts from the works of Somerville and Ross.

The author also gratefully acknowledges the permission granted by William Heinemann Ltd, Publishers, to reprint material from *The Irish Cousins*.

Somerville and Ross

1

Family Backgrounds and the
Beginning of the Collaboration

Anyone who has glanced even cursorily at the map of Ireland, will have noticed how the south-west corner of it has suffered from being the furthest outpost of European resistance to the Atlantic. Winter after winter the fight between sea and rock has raged on, and now, after all these centuries of warfare, the ragged fringe of points and headlands, with long, winding inlets between them, look as though some hungry monster's sharp teeth had torn the soft, green land away, gnawing it out from between the uncompromising lines of rock that stand firm, indigestible and undefeated.

This, the opening paragraph of their second novel, *Naboth's Vineyard* (1891), introduces us to the Somerville and Ross country. A little later in the same work we reach the heart of their territory:

Two tall sycamores, outposts from the Traharta woods, stand in the middle of the street at the foot of the hill, which arches so suddenly above them that the dwellers in the houses half-way up can almost see into the rooks' nests in their topmost branches. These trees—'the Two Trees', as they are affectionately specialized by the people of Rossbrin—are the recognized centre whence radiates all the gossip of the place.

This steep street with its two tall trees in the middle is fictionally situated in the village of Rossbrin. In real life it belongs to the lovely little West Cork village of Castletownshend where the Somerville family have lived since the eighteenth century and where, in 1886, Edith Somerville met her cousin Violet Martin and began a deep friendship which resulted in one of the most celebrated of modern literary partnerships. The future collaborators were second cousins and shared a famous great-grandfather. Their grandmothers, Anna Marie and Katherine Bushe, were both daughters of Charles Kendal Bushe (1767–1843), the celebrated Lord Chief Justice of Ireland whose biography Edith was to write in later life. The Somervilles and the Martins were long-established, Ascendancy, Anglo-Irish families, the former having settled in the far South-West of the country, the latter in the West.

The first Somerville to come to Ireland was an Anglican cleryman who fled from Scotland to Ulster to escape persecution by Covenanters. One of his sons became rector of Castlehaven in Co. Cork. According to Edith (in Ch. IV of *Irish Memories,* 1917):

Somervilles and Townshends had been living and inter-marrying in Castlehaven Parish, with none to molest their ancient solitary reign, since Brian Townshend built himself the fort from which he could look forth upon one of the loveliest harbours in Ireland, and the Reverend

Thomas Somerville, the first of his family to settle in Munster, took to himself (by purchase from the representatives of the Earl of Castlehaven) the old O'Driscoll Castle, and lies buried beside it, in St. Barrahane's churchyard, under a slab that proclaims him to have been "A Worthy Magistrate, and a Safe and Affable Companion."

The house known as "Drishane," which was to become the seat of the Somerville family and where Edith lived for most of her long life, was built by a Thomas Somerville (1725–1793) who made money in shipping. Subsequently the men of the family found their way into the service of the Church or the Crown. Edith's father, Thomas Somerville, was a Colonel of the Buffs and Edith was born on 2 May 1858 on the island of Corfu where her father's regiment was then stationed. The family returned to Ireland from Corfu when Edith was less than a year old. Educated by a series of governesses and, briefly, at Alexandra College, Dublin, Edith early developed an interest in drawing and painting and, as she put it herself, "all her life combined the practice of Painting and Literature with what would seem an equal enthusiasm." When she was in her late teens she spent a term studying at the South Kensington School of Art and, four or five years later, went to Düsseldorf where her cousin (and future brother-in-law), Egerton Coghill, was already studying painting. In 1884 Egerton Coghill moved on to Paris and Edith determined to follow his example, in spite of her family's outraged protests.

In Paris she studied under Colarossi and Délécluse. She also visited for a term the Royal Westminster School

of Art in London. In January 1886, while she was at
home in Castletownshend working on a commission
from *The Graphic* to illustrate three serials, she met
her cousin Violet Martin for the first time.

The importance of this meeting to Edith is evidenced
by the precision with which she recounts it in later life
and by the ardent terms in which she invariably dis-
cusses it. In Ch. X of *Irish Memories* she writes:

> It was, as it happens, in church that I saw her first; in our
> own church, in Castle Townshend. That was on Sunday,
> January 17, 1886.

> It is trite, not to say stupid, to expatiate upon that January
> Sunday when I first met her; yet it has proved the hinge of
> my life, the place where my fate, and hers, turned over,
> and new and unforeseen things began to happen to us.

Violet Florence Martin's family was an ancient one,
of Norman origin. In the sixteenth century a Robert
Martin, High Sheriff and Mayor of Galway, became
possessed of a large amount of land in West Galway,
and in 1590 Ross was his country place. The Crom-
wellian period saw the family, which was Royalist and
Catholic, deprived of its possessions in Galway town but
they held on to all their lands beyond the town of Galway.
Down through the eighteenth century the family remained Catholic in religion and Jacobite in politics.
The first break with the old religion came when Violet's
great-grandfather, Nicholas, turned Protestant to marry
a Protestant neighbor, Elizabeth O'Hara. His six children were born and bred Protestants. However, the
change of religion does not seem to have caused any

friction. Violet's grandfather, Robert Martin, reversed his father's pattern by marrying a Catholic but their four children were brought up in the Protestant faith. Violet herself was a child of her father's second marriage to Anna Selina Fox, granddaughter of Charles Kendal Bushe.

The Martins, in sharp contrast to many of their class, were benevolent landlords who did not follow the normal pattern of absenteeism and rack-renting but lived on their estates and exercised a benevolently feudal control over their large tenantry. Their fortunes declined in the middle of the nineteenth century, the period of the Great Famine during which the Martins did Trojan work in attempting to relieve the dreadful miseries of the Irish poor. Violet's grandfather passed on the estate free of debt but her father, James Martin, lacked his father's business sense and soon had to give evidence before the Land Commission that the Ross estate was burdened with a debt for Poor Rate of £11,000. The political temper of Ireland was also undergoing radical changes and even the amiable paternalism of the Martins of Ross was not immune from the effects. At the election of 1872 the tenants of Ross voted for the Home Rule candidate and, in doing so, directly opposed their landlord who naturally supported the Conservative candidate. The Home Rule candidate, Captain Nolan, was elected by a large majority and James Martin took his tenants' defection as a personal affront. He died shortly after and, a few months later, his son Robert shut up the family house at Ross and went to live in London where he worked as a journalist.

His mother went with the rest of the large family to live in Dublin. Violet was then ten years old. In the ensuing years she largely educated herself. In her affectionate memoir of her brother Robert, subsequently published by Edith as the opening chapter of *Irish Memories,* it is possible to discern a powerful nostalgia for the great days of Ross; and, if the realistically sordid opening of *The Real Charlotte* owes anything to Violet's Dublin life, the contrast between the lost graciousness of Ross and the rigors of the later Dublin period may help to explain, in part at least, the vigor of some of Violet's political views. She remained to the end, in her own phrase, "an Incorrigible Unionist" who detested the emergence in Ireland of those powerful forces which were to bring down in final ruin the landed gentry to whom she herself belonged. With the blunt pragmatism of her class, she summed up the change by asserting that "one indefensible position had been replaced by another, feudal power by clerical." In an interesting exchange of letters with her (included in Ch. XXVII of *Irish Memories*) Stephen Gwynn wrestled with Violet's prejudices, shrewdly pointing out to her:

> You know the peasantry very well; you don't know the middle class. . . . There are plenty of men in Ireland—men of the Nationalist party—brilliant young men, like Kettle, who has also courage and enterprise.

Her reply is a strange mixture of social condescension and political insight:

> . . . no one realizes more than I do the talent and the genius that lie among the Irish lower and middle classes.

I am not quite clear as to what either you or I mean by 'middle classes', I think of well-to-do farmers, and small professional people in the towns. We know both these classes pretty well down here. . . . Last year we had a middle-class business man at luncheon here, an able business man, working like a nigger, and an R.C. and Home Ruler. We discussed the matter. He said, as all you genuine people say and believe, that once Home Rule was granted, the good men among Protestant Unionists would be selected, and the wasters flung aside. I said, and still say, that the brave and fair thing, would be to select them *beforehand*, show trust in them, give them confidence, and then indeed there would be a strong case for Home Rule.

In the same letter she goes on to indicate that what she really fears is what she calls 'the town politicians' and, in a passage oddly reminiscent of W. B. Yeats, she has this to say:

I am not fond of anything about towns; they are full of second-hand thinking; they know nothing of raw material and the natural philosophy of the country people. As to caste, it is in the towns that the *vulgar* idea of caste is created. The country people believe in it strongly; they cling to a belief in what it should stand for of truth and honour—and there the best classes touch the peasant closely, and understand each other.

If we make allowance for the top-dressing of Big House condescension in this, we might almost be listening to a passage from a Yeatsian essay on the affinities between the peasant and the aristocrat.

Edith, though every bit as firmly entrenched in the traditions of her class, nevertheless possessed a geniality and a flexibility lacking in her cousin and was able to come to terms with the new Ireland in a manner impossible to "Martin" (the name by which Edith always referred to her partner). She was well aware of the firmness of Martin's Unionist convictions but believed that, had she been spared, she too would have moved with the times. In Ch. XXVII of *Irish Memories* she confidently asserts:

> Her love of Ireland, combined with her distrust of some of those newer influences in Irish affairs to which her letters refer, made her dread any weakening of the links that bind the United Kingdom into one, but I believe that if she were here now, and saw the changes that the past eighteen months have brought to Ireland, she would be quick to welcome the hope that Irish politics are lifting at last out of the controversial rut of centuries, and that although it has been said of East and West that "never the two shall meet", North and South will yet prove that in Ireland it is always the impossible that happens.

Neither woman had any real grasp of the 'romantic Ireland' so splendidly hymned by Yeats. They never responded imaginatively to the nationalist tradition of Wolfe Tone and Robert Emmet, of John O'Leary and Patrick Pearse. They saw Nationalism of the Irish variety as a combination of Church and agitator to bring down an established order to which they themselves belonged. Grossly unattractive as this oversimplification is in many obvious ways, it is, perhaps, worth pointing out that, in expressing early alarm about the dangers of clerical nationalism, they were merely anticipating the responses of many of their Catholic literary successors. The tone may be different (ascendancy condescension on the one hand, embittered satire on the other) but the focus is recognizably similar.

In writing about Ireland, Violet Martin is often senti-
mentally nostalgic for a system that was at best merely
benevolently paternalistic and at worst brutally autocratic. Edith Somerville, to her credit, had a genuine
sense of the ambivalence the Irish felt toward their
temporary overlords, as this passage from Chapter II
of *Mount Music* (1919) indicates:

> . . . between the eighties and nineties of the nineteenth
> century, the class known as Landed Gentry was still pre-
> eminent in Ireland. Tenants and tradesmen bowed down
> before them, with love sometimes, sometimes with hatred,
> never with indifference. The newspapers of their districts
> recorded their enterprises in marriage, in birth, in death,
> copiously, and with a servile rapture of detail that, though
> it is not yet entirely withheld from their survivors, is now
> bestowed with an equal unction on those who, in many
> instances, have taken their places, geographically, if not
> their place, socially, in Irish every-day existence.

Both women had a quick ear for a telling phrase and
a keen sense of fun. Reared to the correct speech of the
drawing-room and the racy Anglo-Irish of the servants'
hall, they early assumed the freedom of the realms of
the ridiculous thus opened to them in the crevices and
cracks between two languages and two traditions. They
were to become, on their comic side, the hilarious recorders of the brighter part of a dying social framework
and, more sombrely, the acute diagnosticians of the
demise of their own tribe.

Much discussion has centered around the exact nature
of the collaboration between the two writers. Many attempts have been made to define their individual con-

tributions. This curiosity began to manifest itself early, immediately after the publication of their first novel. In Chapter XI of *Irish Memories,* Edith gives the following account of it:

> The question . . . as to which of us held the pen, has ever been considered of the greatest moment, and, as a matter of fact, during our many years of collaboration, it was a point that never entered our minds to consider. To those who may be interested in an unimportant detail, I may say that our work was done conversationally. One or the other—not infrequently both, simultaneously—would state a proposition. This would be argued, combated perhaps, approved or modified; it would then be written down by the (wholly fortuitous) holder of the pen, would be scratched out, scribbled in again; before it found itself finally transferred into decorous Ms. would probably have suffered many things, but it would, at all events, have had the advantage of having been well aired.
>
> I have an interesting letter, written by a very clever woman, herself a writer to a cousin of ours. She found it impossible to believe in the jointness of the authorship, though she admitted her inability to discern the joints in the writing, and having given "An Irish Cousin" a handling far more generous than it deserves, says:
>
> "But though I think the book a success, and cannot pick out the fastenings of the two hands, I yet think the next novel ought to be by *one* of them . . ."
>
> I sent this letter to Martin, and had "the two hands" collaborated in her reply, it could not more sufficingly have expressed my feelings.
>
> V.F.M. to E.Œ.S. (Sept. 1889)
>
> "You do not say if you want Miss ———'s most interesting letter back. Never mind what she says about people writing together. We have proved that we can do it, and we shall go on. The reason few people can is because they have separate minds upon most subjects, and fight their own hands all the time. I think the two Shockers have a very strange belief in each other, joined to a critical faculty;

added to which, writing together is, to me at least, one of the greatest pleasures I have. To write with you doubles the triumph and the enjoyment, having first halved the trouble and anxiety."

When Violet visited Scotland at the beginning of 1895, after the publication of *The Real Charlotte* (1894), she encountered Andrew Lang as a fellow dinner guest at St. Andrews and was quizzed by him about the mystery of the twin authorship of the novels. She mentions the incident in a letter to Edith:

> To me then Andrew L. with a sort of off-hand fling,
> "I suppose you're the one that did the writing?"
> I explained with some care that it was not so. He said he didn't know how any two people could equally evolve characters, etc., that *he* had tried, and it was always he or the other who did it all. I said I didn't know how we managed, but anyhow that I know little of bookmaking as a science.

Edith's nephew, Sir Patrick Coghill, has given an interesting first-hand account of his aunts at work. He confirms Edith's assertion that their work tended to begin conversationally and that it proceeded on a basis of mutuality, never separately. When he moves from discussion of the mechanical side of the matter to an attempt at definition of the nature of their separate contributions, he suggests that Edith may have supplied "the larger part of the motive power, Martin most of the cutting and polishing." He, further, compares the work they achieved together with the work done by Edith after her cousin's death in 1915 and suggests that the tighter control over form in the earlier work and the larger canvas adopted by Edith in the later novels would tend to suggest that, while Edith may have supplied a greater share of the matter, Violet probably exercised more control over the form of the books.

The comparison of the pre-1915 work with the post-1915 work is, of course, the one which most readily suggests itself in any attempt at discrimination between the two hands. It is sometimes suggestive, though probably fundamentally unfair to Edith. Any successful literary collaboration is by its very nature greater than the sum of its parts. Edith Somerville and Violet Martin established between them a unique rapport, based on their deep love for each other, their common backgrounds, shared interests, and intimately related responses to experience. Together, they struck sparks from each other constantly. Sometimes these sparks ignited a blaze of achievement, as in *The Real Charlotte;* sometimes they crackled busily and brightly, as in the "R.M." stories. But to find the source of the spark in the flint rather than in the striker is surely unfair. It is possible to suggest that many of the effective descriptive scenes are the result of Edith's painter's eye, that the profounder moral insights came from Violet's keener intellect. Specific scenes may be ascribed to one writer rather than the other: the opening chapter of *The Real Charlotte* traced, perhaps, direct to Violet's Dublin childhood. Lady Dysart of Bruff may be Edith's affectionately satirical version of her own idiosyncratic mother. We may go further and opine that Violet would scarcely have tolerated some of the more heavy-handed jocosities of Edith's later work, but any such conclusions must be, of their nature, oversimplifications. Maurice Collis, in his biography, clearly indicates his belief that Violet was the real writer of the pair and that Edith is hardly worthy of serious literary consideration once her companion has left her. Violet Powell is closer to the real truth of the matter and more sensitively alive to the complexities of a unique partnership when she comments:

> In their writing together Edith contributed her full share of wit, and perhaps more than her full share of physical energy, a quality often overlooked as an essential to the practice of literature, but she dug less deeply than Martin into the lodes of human experience.
>
> —Ch. XV, *The Irish Cousins*

When she was nearing her ninetieth year, Edith was still trying to satisfy her readers' curiosity on the question of joint authorship. Her conclusions, expressed in her last published article, in *Irish Writing* (1946), were becomingly modest:

> I believe I am right in attributing to my Cousin the more subtle and recondite adjective, the more knife-edged slice of sarcasm, the more poetic feeling for words, and a sense of Style that seems to me flawless and unequalled. And I believe that possibly my profession as a painter, has helped and developed my feeling for colour, and sense of form, and the privileges conferred by horses and hounds (and beloved little fox-terriers) have brought all these things specially near to me.
>
> But our reliance on one another, whether on this plane or another, is what can never be explained. There have been many empty moments, long spaces of silence, both grappling with the same intangible idea. Sometimes the compelling creative urge would come on both, and we

would try to reconcile the two impulses, searching for a form into which best to cast them—one releasing it, perhaps as a cloudy suggestion, to be caught up by the other, and given form and colour, then to float away in a flash of certainty, a completed sentence—as two dancers will yield to the same impulse, given by the same strain of music, and know the joy of shared success.

It was, I suppose, because of that fundamental sympathy of which I have spoken, that in spite of practical difficulties, and sometimes of inevitable divergences of opinion, in all the happy years of our working and living together, there was never a break in the harmony of our work, nor a flaw in our mutual understanding.

2
Early Novels and Travel Books

The cousins embarked upon their first novel in a spirit of fun, sounding from the outset the purposefully amateur note which was to impart to their work its distinctively carefree quality, and ultimately, perhaps, deprive it of the sort of practical determination that compels writers to their highest flights. Both had already done some writing. Edith had published a short story in the *Argosy* and Violet had had an article on Poor Relief in the *Irish Times*. They had thought of writing journalistic articles together, with Edith as illustrator. Work on *An Irish Cousin* began late in 1887 to the accompaniment of a chorus of family derision. The book was referred to by their jeering relatives as "The Shocker," since in its original conception it was to resemble the "Shilling Shockers"—light books of a thrilling nature then much in vogue. However, a more serious purpose manifested itself to the new authors in the course of their work on the book. This was brought about by a visit to an old kinswoman, which Edith describes in considerable detail. This old lady lived alone in an old house:

> . . . it was the old house, dying even then, that touched our imaginations; full of memories of brave days past. . . .
> The sunset was red in the west when our horses were brought round to the door, and it was at this precise moment that into the Irish Cousin some thrill of genuineness was breathed. In the darkened facade of the long grey house, a window, just over the hall-door caught our attention. In it, for an instant, was a white face. . . .
> . . . We had been warned of certain subjects not to be approached, and knew enough of the history of that old house to realise what we had seen. An old stock, isolated from the world at large, wearing itself out in those excesses that are a protest of human nature against unnatural conditions, dies at last with its victims round its death-bed.
> The shock of it was what we needed, and with it "the Shocker" started into life, or, if that is too much to say for it, its authors, at least felt that conviction had come to them—the insincere ambition of the "Penny Dreadful" faded, realities asserted themselves, and the faked "thrills" that were to make our fortunes were repudiated for ever. Little as we may have achieved it, an ideal of Art rose then for us, far and faint as the half-moon, and often, like her, hidden in clouds, yet never quite lost or forgotten.
> —Ch. XI, *Irish Memories*

They had, in fact, at the very outset of their collaboration, defined their literary role and realized that they were to be the recorders of the decline of their own kind, taking their place in the tradition of the Ascendancy novel inaugurated by Maria Edgeworth in *Castle Rackrent*. Thus, *An Irish Cousin* is, as Edith herself suggests, a blend of the absurdly romantic and the convincingly realistic. The heroine, Theo Sarsfield, returns from Canada to her dead father's Irish home at Durrus in an atmosphere compounded of equal parts of Brontean Gothic, Le Fanu-like mystification, and Rackrentish disorder. The house is old and creaky with windowpanes broken in the best Edgeworth manner, with sleek, well-fed horses housed in dreadfully neglected stables. There is even a local madwoman, Moll Hourihane, who mops and mows outside Theo's window in a manner reminiscent of the celebrated Mme. Rougierre in Sheridan Le Fanu's *Uncle Silas*. The uncle of this novel is Theo's father's brother Dominick, like Uncle Silas a mysterious mixture of courtesy and aloofness and, like him, guilty of a crime against his own flesh and blood. All the horror and mystification are finally explained away rather easily and what we remember with pleasure is the novel's account of the day-to-day life of the Irish gentry. We dismiss Uncle Dominick and mad Moll and recall with delight Mrs. Jackson-Croly's roistering dance and the Moycullen hunt. In Theo's cousin Willy we encounter a well-executed first draft of Flurry Knox of the "R.M." stories. The heroine is a combination of Violet's and Edith's images of themselves—pretty, determined, a great rider to hounds, excited by the rigors of the chase. The love interest is slight and poorly handled. Affection the writers can manage but passion defeats them. Everywhere we see a social novel struggling to break through the book's overlay of Irish Gothic.

An Irish Cousin was completed in May 1888 and was offered to Messrs. Sampson Low who rejected it without comment. In December of that year Richard Bentley & Son delighted the new authors by accepting the book. Bentleys offered them £25 on publication and £25 on sale of 500 copies and they delightedly accepted. The novel appeared in August of the following year with Edith's identity concealed under the improbable pseudonym of "Geilles Herring," which she did not employ again, and Violet appearing as "Martin Ross," the literary identity she retained until the end. *An Irish Cousin* received generally favorable reviews and soon went into a second edition. In the meantime the writers had begun work on their next novel.

Naboth's Vineyard, which had what Edith later described as "a preliminary canter" as a short-story entitled "Slide Number 42" in the 1890 Christmas number of the *Lady's Pictorial,* was to be the only full-length work in which the partners dealt with Irish village life. In doing so, they were gallantly trying to depict lives which they could know only from the outside. In its penetration of character the book is at best an honorable failure. In construction it marks an advance on their first novel. It has a sureness, a speed and a directness lacking in *An Irish Cousin* and is altogether less circuitous. A tightly controlled story is told with some force. As it opens we find Harriet Donovan married to a wealthy gombeen-man, John Donovan, and bitterly regretting her earlier rejection of the handsome Rick O'Grady. The latter, now a successful businessman himself, is in love with Ellen Leonard, daughter of a widow who has taken over the tenancy of a farm boycotted by the Land League. Donovan exploits his position as President of the local branch of the League to bring pressure to bear on the widow Leonard, in an effort

to drive her off the farm he covets. Rick O'Grady comes
to the aid of the Leonards but incurs the jealous hatred
of Dan Hurley, who also loves Ellen Leonard. Hurley
plans to murder his rival but Donovan falls into his
trap and is killed instead.

The novel's weakness is that the people are observed
from outside, without much real sympathy. They are
lay figures who act as they do because they lack educa-
tion and breeding, and instinct is their only guide. One
has no sense of growth or development in any of the
characters, who are simply pawns to be moved towards
a prepared end. The plotting is tighter than in *An
Irish Cousin* but there is no inwardness, no real exploration of character or motive. John Donovan is
greedy but his original involvement with Dan Hurley's
mother (whom he drove into an insane asylum) is
largely unexplained. In the encounter between Harriet
Donovan and Rick O'Grady, at which she warns him
that he is in danger from the Land League, we get
the following revealing comment:

> She made the mistake that a woman in a higher class of
> life would not have made in a similar case—she thought
> she had frightened him about his own personal safety.

The assumption underlying this is that vulgarity and
stupidity are qualities proper to the poor. Harriet's action is here explained in terms of her social class, in a
deplorable over-simplification. This lapse is the more
regrettable in view of her real sexual force and com-
plexity, which are at times convincingly portrayed. Her
hungry desire for Rick O'Grady, the lover she has

earlier spurned, is a preparation for Charlotte Mullen's
sullen lusting after Roderick Lambert. Her encounters
with her husband (e.g. Chapters VIII and XVI) are
strongly depicted and accurately observed.

One sees in this novel the first stirrings of the writers'
great interest in the strikingly descriptive phrase. A
wizened child is likened to "a creature like a Japanese
caricature of a frog." Edith's pictorial sense comes
through powerfully in a fine description of the mackerel
salting, in Chapter XIV:

> There was a line of tables up the middle of the pier, each
> with its paraffin lamp smoking and flaring in the partial
> shelter of a fish-box, and each with its wild, Rembrandtish
> group of women splitting the innumerable mackerel, and
> rubbing lavish fistfuls of coarse gray salt into each, before
> it was flung to the men to be packed into barrels. The
> lamps shone fantastically on the double row of intent faces,
> on the quickly moving arms of the women, crimsoned to
> the elbows, on the tables, varnished with the same colour,
> and on the cold silvery heaps of fish.

The novel honestly tries to convey some of the complexities and contradictions of the Irish political scene,
with the Land League boycotting farms which have
been vacated by rack-rented tenants and local profiteers
making the most of the opportunities offered to them
by a pretense of patriotism. Edith was, in later life,
similarly to attempt to depict the political and agrarian
complexities of the new Ireland in *An Enthusiast*
(1921).

Naboth's Vineyard has an unconvincingly melodramatic ending in which Dan Hurley, having shaken

hands with the dead Donovan, has an epileptic fit and dies, and the passionate Harriet Donovan is made to immure herself improbably in a convent. The writers fall back on melodramatic contrivance to tidy up the destinies of characters who have been set in motion but never really explored. Such strength as this novel possesses lies in its vivid descriptions of woods and streams, of lonely country places and bustling village life. The partners are here displaying their sense of locality which is going to be of such importance in *The Real Charlotte*. That remarkable book appeared in 1894 and is so marvellous an advance on their previous work that one wonders at the brevity of their apprenticeship. In it they suddenly found their real métier, moving from a melodrama they no longer needed to the realism they had been groping for and from an Irish Catholic setting they scarcely understood to a Protestant Ascendancy world which nobody has understood better.

"Tours, Idle Tours" was the title given by Edith to the next phase of their joint literary experience. It describes the period 1890–93, during which they made a number of journeys, which they wrote up in the form of descriptive articles for periodicals. Most of the material subsequently appeared also in book form.

The first tour was undertaken in 1890 and it took them to Connemara. The articles first appeared in *The Lady's Pictorial* and the subsequent book, *Through Connemara in a Governess Cart,* was published in 1892. It is trivial stuff enough, carefully tailored for the genteel readers of a London women's magazine. One soon wearies of repeated accounts of the idiosyncrasies of the

jennet, Sibbie, hired to draw the governess cart in which
the pair travelled and, in general, one retains from the
book an impression of damp and misty discomfort. In a
revealing early passage, the travellers describe how

> . . . the first vision of the long Recess dinner-table dissipated
> all our hopes of the comic squalor that is endured gladly
> for the sake of its literary value . . .

They actually went to the lengths of inventing the
"comic squalor" which they failed to find, in the account of the night spent in the cottage of the widow
Joyce (Chs. V and VI). There is no mention of this
incident in the writers' diaries and it was presumably
invented to brighten a narrative which might otherwise
have seemed unduly concerned with mountains, mists
and jennets. Edith is the narrator throughout and she
tries to introduce some stylistic variety by the mildly
comic depiction of "my second cousin" who, as a native
of the countryside through which they are travelling,
undertakes to advise on inevitably disastrous shortcuts,
loses her hat in a high wind and is generally made a
mild butt throughout as she peers shortsightedly
through her pince-nez and tugs impotently at the reins.
Though the writers assert their Irishness, contrasting
themselves with all the other tourists who are English,
the tone throughout is that of two "quality" ladies
abroad in a backward land where the only evidences of
civilization are traceable to the influence of occasional
English visitors. It is good-natured, potboiling stuff of
a superficial kind. It does not pretend to profundity
and need not be lingered over.

Much the same might be said of the account of a trip which they took to Bordeaux in the autumn of 1891, again on behalf of *The Lady's Pictorial,* for the purpose of writing about the vineyards of the area. The book, entitled *In the Vine Country,* was published in 1893. (Martin had first suggested the cumbersomely jocose title *From Cork to Claret* but the publishers rejected it.)

This time they had to cope with the heat and the insects rather than with the Connemara rains, but, in broad outline, their account of their adventures takes a familiar form. They protest their unfamiliarity with the details of viticulture, speak bad French to the natives and make surreptitious cups of tea on the spirit stove in their hotel bedroom in the same mood of school-girlish bonhomie as before. They stay the night in the cottage of a French peasant woman and the incident parallels the night in the cottage of the Widow Joyce almost to a flea. Later they are restored to their proper role as "ladies of quality" when, as a result of an introduction, they are shown over the vineyards of a wealthy owner and entertained at tea in his country house. Subsequently they are guests of Mr. Gilbey at the Château Loudenne, where they find that English wealth properly applied to a French château is much to their taste. They watch the treading of the grapes, reluctantly taste the *moût,* attend a *fin de vendange* dance, taste the *vendangeurs'* soup and *ragoût* and generally enjoy themselves as brief tourists and chatty commentators. They seem to have enjoyed their fortnight in France.

The third tour was undertaken after the completion

of *The Real Charlotte,* while arrangements for the novel's publication were still being held up. The trip, a riding tour of North Wales, was commissioned by *Black and White* but the articles eventually appeared in *Blackwoods.* The book, *Beggars on Horseback,* was published in 1895. On this occasion, the pen is in Martin's hand and Edith figures in the narrative as Miss O'Flannigan, the artist. Their horses, called Tommy and Tom, take them from Welshpool to Dolgelly. They stay at various Welsh inns, attend a Welsh-language church service, press on and climb Snowdon, on top of which they spend a night in great discomfort. They suffer various mishaps with their temperamental mounts, turn up at Plas Newydd on a Sunday, when the celebrated home of the Ladies of Llangollen is unhappily closed to visitors, and finally travel back to Welshpool by train with the horses. The writing is brisker this time. The narrative moves with greater speed and the jokes, when they come, are less labored. The amiable jocosity of the earlier tour journals is replaced by what almost amounts to curt dismissiveness. No great affection for the land of Snowdon and tin tabernacles is conveyed.

The last of these tours was undertaken on behalf of *The Lady's Pictorial* later in the same year, 1893. It took the partners to Denmark. The articles, under the title *In the State of Denmark,* were subsequently included by Edith in the volume *Strayaways* (1920) in the Preface to which she commented as follows:

Of the chapters that describe our wanderings "In the State of Denmark", it may be said that they are often written as it were from the point of view of Martin Ross (who did, in fact, write the larger share of them) , and the curious in such matters may, should they so desire, compare them with other of her writings that I have reprinted here, and may, perhaps, discern something of her individual outlook in many of them.

As has already been suggested, differentiating between the two pens can be a risky business but it is certainly true that the account of the Danish tour is much less leisurely and self-indulgent than the earlier accounts of their travels in France and the west of Ireland. The pace is closer to that of *Beggars on Horseback,* where Martin also held the pen. The narrative moves swiftly and economically. Sentences are often long and complex, packed with information. There is much detailed observation and no protestations of amateurish incompetence in matters of technical detail such as speckled some of the earlier journals. There is a sense of an almost nervous determination to pack in as much as possible both in the way of personal adventure and observation. The light-hearted tone of the earlier travel books is here varied by frequent, realistic touches reminiscent of similar effects in the fine novel on which they had so recently been engaged. As the travellers set out from Liverpool Street, a German-Jewish family party arrives to share their carriage. The mother is an invalid and the family is in great distress at the parting. The scene is rapidly and honestly sketched, not milked of its significance but left to produce its own resonances. One is reminded of the effectively realistic depiction of Charlotte Mullen at the bedside of her dying aunt. Elsewhere too, there are frequent touches of an unusual kind. During one of their social calls, Ibsen is the topic of conversation and the report of the matter is pleasantly serious without being ponderous:

> Ibsen was the topic that grew and prospered in the pleasant atmosphere; a fruitful topic at all times in Denmark, and sure to be treated there with a sanity and a temperateness born, it must be, of innate knowledge of Ibsen's country, his language, his people, frequently of Ibsen himself. He does not seem to startle these neighbours of his; they appreciate strongly, they condemn vigorously, but there is no discordant outcry of tongues newly versed in Ibsenese, no fever and jerk of initiation, no enthusiastic flourishing of new brooms. There appears little attempt to claim for him a meaning beyond the simple reproduction of character and action; he himself claims no more than this, and would not, so we were told, support in any way the theories of those who will not leave unexpounded even the dolls of the Master-Builder's wife.
>
> —Ch. XIV, *Strayaways*

This, like the later discussion of the sculptor Thorwaldsen, sounds like Martin rather than the often purposefully uncritical Edith. Martin's distinctive tone comes through also in her brief comments on her companion, which are more acidulous than Edith's affectionately satirical reflections on 'my second cousin' in the earlier tour books. Martin's sharp eye and sharper tongue pin down Edith unforgettably for us as she flourishes at a Danish dinner-table:

> . . . the pointed moustache of my cousin's companion was twitching in the assiduity of his conversation, and she herself was evidently saying "Vraiment!" with a gesture whose Parisian *abandon* had yet in it some unconscious touch of the Skibereen apple-woman.
>
> —Ch. XIV, *Strayaways*

It is amusing to notice how the cousins make the most of their dual nationality while they are abroad and oddly pleasing to see them having, as it were, the best of both parts of their broken, Ascendancy world. When Violet is accidentally separated from Edith during their train journey in Germany, she becomes "an English lady" in distress and is thus described in the messages sent after her by the agitated Edith. Clearly, when one is intent on impressing German officials, the value of the British connection cannot be over-estimated. However, later on, when they have safely arrived in Denmark, Martin reflects amusingly on the advantages of "being Irish":

> It was natural that Ibsen's women should induce comparison with Englishwomen, who, perhaps by their own fault, seem so badly understood by the foreigner, so insulated into a theory. It was not, of course, their shortcomings of which we heard most, yet some slight consciousness of reservation, hardly amounting to disparagement, made us glad we were Irish. There is nothing aggressively superior about being Irish—at least, other people do not think so, and however that may be, there is a sense of kinship between the Irish and those who are not English that is curious, yet unmistakeable. Taking this into consideration, we ventured to hope that it was intended as a compliment when we were assured that we were quite unlike the English, but it was not altogether so gratifying to discover subsequently that Englishwomen were specially remarkable for their rich and handsome clothes.
>
> —Ch. XIV, *Strayaways*

All in all, this is much the most solid and most interesting of the tour journals and it is, perhaps, surprising that it was the only one not done into book form at a later date.

3

The Real Charlotte *(1894)*
and The Silver Fox *(1897)*

In October 1889, Richard Bentley, evidently impressed by the good reception of *An Irish Cousin,* wrote to the authors to suggest that they should write a three-volume novel for him. He offered £100 down and £125 on the second 500 copies. They were then working on *Naboth's Vineyard,* the rights of which they subsequently sold outright to a clerical acquaintance, the Rev. Frederick Longbridge, for £35. According to Edith's account of the matter in Chapter XVIII of *Irish Memories,* the partners were so gratified by the serious reception accorded to their second novel that they resolved to plunge straightway into the three-volume novel requested by Bentley. A beginning was made at Ross during November 1889 but other commitments, among them several of the travel books, intervened and work on the serious novel was suspended for a time. They returned to it at Drishane in April of the following year, wrote the opening chapter and again abandoned the novel for the moment. At the end of that year they completed a further five chapters but the book was not finished until the early summer of 1892. An entry in Edith's diary for June 8 reads:

> Wrote feverishly. The most agitating scenes of Charlotte. Finished Francie.

Revisions undertaken in the course of recopying the manuscript and further interruptions saw to it that *The Real Charlotte* (which had begun its life under the title *The Welsh Aunt*) was not finally ready for submission until February 1893.

Bentley offered £100 which was indignantly refused. The work was next offered to Smith and Elder who turned it down. Negotiations were then opened with Ward and Downey to whom *The Real Charlotte* was finally sold for £250 and half American rights. The book appeared in May of the following year and got good reviews from the *Athenaeum, Pall Mall* and the *National Observer*. It was disliked by the reviewer in the *Westminster Gazette* and, for a time at least, by the authors' own relatives, who tended to find the book sordid and gloomy.

The novel is without question the writers' finest achievement. Edith's account of its genesis would seem to suggest that this was the first work in which they took themselves seriously as writers and the book everywhere bears witness to this new confidence. For the first time they move from the safe but artistically unexciting regions of melodrama and stereotype to the exploration of character and motive in a carefully realized setting. The resultant work is a splendid piece of realistic fiction which blossoms into a definitive exploration of what one critic has called "the Indian summer of the Anglo-Irish Ascendancy."

At the book's centre is Charlotte Mullen herself, the only figure directly borrowed from real life. She is a splendidly realized and entirely convincing figure of evil, the book's machiavel whose contrivings bring upon others a ruin from which she is not herself exempt. Charlotte is the daughter of the former agent for the Dysart estates. She is a middle-aged, ugly, passionate woman who nurses a secret desire for Roderick Lambert, her father's successor as agent. Her principal victim is her young cousin, Francie Fitzpatrick, the "butterfly" whose insouciant flittings through the novel's complex events contrast so effectively with Charlotte's malign schemings. Charlotte's manipulation of events begins early, with her decision to repudiate her dying aunt's bequest to Francie. She plans to marry Francie to Christopher, the Dysart heir, but Francie unwittingly thwarts her by falling in love with Captain Hawkins, a military man whose regiment is briefly stationed in Lismoyle. After the death of Mrs. Lambert, Charlotte has hopes of marrying Roderick Lambert but, again, Francie, whose affair with Hawkins has gone wrong and who has incredibly chosen to reject Christopher Dysart, steps into Charlotte's path by marrying Lambert herself. Charlotte's progress through the book is a sequence of successes in all her business dealings and a series of insulting failures in the personal passion which matters so much more. Lambert, whose robust virility always attracts her, is contemptuously aware of his power over her but chooses to exercise it as a lever for borrowing money from her when he needs it. Thus, as Charlotte Mullen is developed in the course of the novel, she becomes at once loathsome and oddly pathetic. She is ugly and intelligent: Francie is beautiful and feather-brained. Charlotte wants Roderick: Francie casually accepts him merely to teach Hawkins a lesson. Charlotte aspires to social contact with the Dysarts: Francie unbelievably refuses to marry Christopher Dysart. The capable, contriving Charlotte can acquire the farm of the ruined Julia Duffy, she can control Lambert's financial affairs, she can even murder his wife; but all her seeming efficiency goes for naught in the matter closest to the hidden heart of the "real" Charlotte. The book develops into an effective exposé of the essential irrelevance of evil. Charlotte is a figure of Faustian stature who can do everything except what she most desires.

The novel is delightfully written, in prose of an Austenian tautness and resilience. It abounds in memorable scenes. Even the animals who appear are made to play an effective part, devoid for once of that embarrassing anthropomorphic coyness with which they are sometimes endowed in the writers' other work. The world of Lismoyle is brought to vivid life, with the Dysart family aristocratically presiding over its social destinies, and a host of lesser figures living in their shadow. The ragbag quality of the society is brilliantly conveyed right at the beginning, in the depiction of Lady Dysart's tennis-party. The writers are so brilliantly in control here that the scene is made, at once, to amuse us, to inform us effortlessly of the relevant social distinctions and to acquaint us intimately with the characters of Charlotte Mullen, Lady Dysart and Roderick Lambert. The encounter between Lady Dysart and Charlotte is particularly effective:

> 'How do you do, Miss Mullen?' she said in tones of unconcealed gloom. 'Have you ever seen so few men in your life? and there are five and forty women! I cannot imagine where they have all come from, but I know where I wish they would take themselves to, and that is to the bottom of the lake!'
>
> . . . Charlotte understood that nothing personal was intended; she knew that the freedom of Bruff had been given to her . . .
>
> "Well, your ladyship," she said, in the bluff, hearty voice which she felt accorded best with the theory of herself that she had built up in Lady Dysart's mind, 'I'll head a forlorn hope to the bottom of the lake for you, and welcome; but for the honour of the house you might give me a cup o' tay first!'
>
> Charlotte had many tones of voice, according with the many facets of her character, and when she wished to be playful she affected a vigorous brogue, not perhaps being aware that her own accent scarcely admitted of being strengthened.
>
> This refinement of humour was probably wasted on Lady Dysart. She was an Englishwoman, and, as such, was constitutionally unable to discern perfectly the subtle grades of Irish vulgarity.
>
> —Ch. III, *The Real Charlotte*

This exchange between the two women is, on the comic plane, revealingly analogous to the central drift of the novel. Charlotte, in a gauche presumption of mutuality, prepares for Lady Dysart's amusement a piece of stage-Irish histrionics which goes unremarked by her listener. Her comic contrivances here are seen to be irrelevant, just as her more malign contrivances elsewhere in the novel are finally placed in a similar way. Charlotte's image of herself in Lady Dysart's mind and the latter's serene indifference to it are a sort of moral paradigm of the book's pattern. Charlotte's supple self-knowledge here is just as irrelevant as all her devious scheming. The fabric of the book is tightly woven throughout.

From its light-hearted opening in the sunny sordidness of the north side of Dublin to its tragic end, the novel abounds in vivid scenes which throb with life and all serve both to enrich the story and, at the same time, implement the plot. Charlotte's introduction to us is achieved in the gloomy setting of her aunt's deathchamber. There broods over the chapter an atmosphere of sordid menace. The depiction of Charlotte herself is daringly repulsive:

Miss Charlotte gave the fire a frugal poke, and lit a candle in the flame provoked from the sulky coals. In doing so some ashes became embedded in the grease, and taking a hair-pin from the ponderous mass of brown hair that was piled on the back of her head, she began to scrape the candle clean. Probably at no moment of her forty years of life had Miss Charlotte Mullen looked more startlingly plain than now, as she stood, her squat figure draped in a magenta flannel dressing-gown, and the candle light shining upon her face. The night of watching had left its traces upon even her opaque skin. The lines about her prominent mouth and chin were deeper than usual; her broad

cheeks had a flabby pallor; only her eyes were bright and
untired, and the thick yellow-white hand that manipulated
the hair-pin was deft as it was wont to be.

—Ch. II, *The Real Charlotte*

So Charlotte enters our awareness, squat, ugly, capable,
and provided with a menacing familiar in the person
of a tom-cat perversely named Susan. It is correct that
our first glimpse of her should show her with her guard
down, in the presence of a dying woman who has no
power to harm her any more. Subsequently, we shall be
seeing many faces of Charlotte as she vulgarly rallies
Lady Dysart, chaffs Roderick Lambert or dupes his unhappy wife, cozens Francie or manipulates the wretched
Julia Duffy.

The writers set in motion for us the sort of society
they themselves had grown up in and knew with rare
intimacy. The Dysarts are an engaging group of aris-
tocratic hybrids. Lady Dysart, as amiably and vaguely
autocratic as Mrs Somerville who was her prototype, is
depicted as the well-intentioned, totally uncomprehending Englishwoman adrift in an Ireland she likes but
does not understand. She asks too many women to her
tennis party, tries ineffectually to marry her son to an
English heiress and plants her flower-beds full of the
chickweed plants which she has mistaken for asters. Her
husband, Sir Benjamin, is a choleric invalid, trapped in
a wheelchair, an absurd creature of diminishing menace
who is wheeled about, appropriately imprisoned, by his
Irish attendant James Canavan. Pamela, his daughter,
is a well-meaning, well-mannered girl who sings in the
choir, worries about her mother's guests and is plainly

doomed to spinsterdom. Christopher, the son and heir, is introspective, ineffective and unsuccessful in his wooing of Francie. Together they represent a composite picture of sterility and decay at the top of the social hierarchy.

The book is passionately concerned with rank and social status. Around and beneath the Dysarts we encounter the other people of the novel: Roderick Lambert, who attains "brevet rank as a country gentleman" by virtue of his position as agent for the Dysart estates; Charlotte Mullen, daughter of a school-teacher, clawing her way up the social ladder and multiplying her possessions as she goes; the Lismoyle mamas and their hopeful daughters; the visiting military whose colourful presence adds bustle and life to the village and to the book; Lambert's pathetic "turkey-hen" of a wife; Francie, pretty, carefree and doomed. The halcyon heyday of the Anglo-Irish Ascendancy is evoked with almost overpowering nostalgia. There are boat trips with handsome officers, tennis parties, hilarious amateur theatricals, flirtations in sunny arbors, catty conversations at tea-parties. Somewhere in the background is the dark hinterland of the Irish poor. We have access to it through Charlotte who returns to Ferry Row (the book's "Mixen Lane") to collect her rents for filthy cottages and her interest on loans. The people she meets there respect and fear her, as does Dinny Lydon, the tailor who is turning a coat for her and whom she intimidates by her knowledge of the Irish language as well as by her general ferocity.

Francie enters the world of Lismoyle from the precarious, middle-class world of Dublin which is briefly but effectively depicted in the novel's opening chapter and, again, in Chapter XXXVI, when, like Jane Austen's Fanny Price, Francie returns from the splendors and comforts of the aristocracy to the drabness of her mother's unfashionable holiday home. The crawling embarrassments of Francie's visit to the Dysarts at Bruff are meticulously rendered. Everywhere in this novel, the partners write with a fine grace and a perception for which the two earlier novels have done little to prepare us. They have, quite literally, "come home" and have written out of full hearts about a world in whose essence their lives are steeped. So faithful is their depiction that wise judgment attends on but does not impede their representation. There are no crude over-simplifications such as sometimes occur elsewhere in the work of these writers. Class distinctions certainly matter enormously but they are not, in this novel, made morally decisive. Lady Dysart herself behaves with crashing vulgarity in her encounter with Christopher during which he tells her of his incredible rejection by Francie. Charlotte Mullen, as villain, is all the more convincing in that her rage and jealousy sometimes push her into taking risks to gratify a temporary spite. This is unquestionably the finest Irish novel of the nineteenth century and there are not all that many in the twentieth to challenge its primacy.

The Silver Fox (1897), the cousins' first full-length novel after *The Real Charlotte,* is shorter than its predecessor and, by comparison, a disappointing performance. Edith herself pointed out one of the reasons for this disappointment:

> It had the disadvantage, from our point of view, of appearing first in a weekly paper (since defunct). This involved a steady rate of production, and recurring "curtains," which are alike objectionable; the former to the peace of mind of the author, while the latter are noxious trucklings to and stimulation of the casual reader. That, at least, is how the stipulated sensation at the end of each weekly instalment appeared to us at the time, and I have seen no reason for relinquishing these views.
> —Ch. XXII, *Irish Memories*

The insistence on regular climaxes for purposes of serial gratification probably accounts for the book's lack of coherence. Short though it is, it is diffuse and lacking in sharpness of focus. It is one of those irritating works in the course of which the reader constantly finds himself led into the belief that he has at last fathomed the writer's object only to have his dawning comprehension muffled yet again in vagueness and indirections. At times the novel seems to be tackling a favorite theme of the writers, the English adrift in an Ireland they do not understand. Wilfrid Glasgow, the engineer who is engaged on driving an ill-fated railway through unsuitable country, and Lady Susan French, stylish and very English, are the two foreigners who, in their respective ways, come up against the puzzling facts and fancies of Irish life. Glasgow runs into trouble with Irish superstition and, on a more mundane level, Irish labor. Lady Susan, who flirts unconvincingly with him, is a more vigorous version of Miss Hope-Drummond from *The*

Real Charlotte, the wealthy Englishwoman abroad in a confusing country whose natives speak a version of her language and comport themselves in a fashion which seems intermittently familiar but ultimately incomprehensible. Slaney Morris is the Irishwoman of the piece, contrasting with Lady Susan in her role of "clever provincial" made to seem gauche by the smartness of the English set but secretly scornful of their "screaming inanities." She is supplied with an unlikely beau and eventual husband in the person of the unhappily named Bunbury and the various romances, flirtations and misunderstandings are wrapped up in a mélange of Irish superstition centering around a mysterious silver fox and a local legend. The fox never really becomes a convincing figure of menace and the peasant sub-plot never blends satisfactorily with the rest of the story. The book blunders on through misunderstandings and melodramatic contrivance to a confused climax in the hunting field where the writers try desperately to gather together the unhappily disparate strands of their muddled narrative.

The book abounds in irritating improbabilities. The sensitive, intellectual Slaney is married off to the bumbling Bunbury; the arrogant Lady Susan is made to fall in love eventually with her miserably uninteresting husband; a Cockney wife is produced out of nowhere for Wilfrid Glasgow. The characters are mere stereotypes, never explored or developed in any convincing fashion. The best thing in the book is the realistic description of Danny Quin's wake in the second chapter. This is entirely convincing and must surely owe much to Violet Martin's fascinated interest in such scenes, as evidenced by letters she wrote to Edith from Ross in 1895 (letters from which Edith quotes extensively in Ch. XVII of *Irish Memories*). The handling of this scene is impeccably accurate and has a truth, compounded of direct observation and wry comment, which Synge might have been glad to achieve. The vigorous, peasant speech is a preparation for the linguistic brio of the R.M. stories. The book wakes to brief life during this chapter with such exchanges as the following:

> "A nice, dacent little man as ever was in the barony," said an old woman glibly; "the Lord have mercy on him, 'tis he got the death very sudden"—she crossed herself—"and very quare, the Lord save us."
> "I understand," said the publican, conscious of leading the conversation with ability, "that he sustained fatal injuries from a fall."
> "Arrah, what fatal injuries!" returned the old woman with scorn; "no, but to break his neck was what he done. Didn't he walk out over the brink o' the big sand-pit in Cashel the same as one that wouldn't have the sighth, an' he a fine soople man no more than seventy years? 'Twas like a reelin' in the head the crayture got."

The old woman's downright rejection of the publican's colorless cliché and her substitution of a racy and vigorous alternative version is one of the few bright spots in an otherwise disappointing book.

4

Some Experiences of an Irish R.M. (1899) *and* Further Experiences of an Irish R.M. (1908)

In the summer of 1898 Edith and Martin went on holiday to Étaples where Edith painted busily and Martin helped by beating off intrusive French children who tried to steal the paints and jostle the artist. It was during this holiday that the "R.M." stories, which were to bring them international fame, were first conceived. For several years prior to this they had been writing stories for various London magazines, including the *Badminton Magazine, Black and White* and *The Lady's Pictorial,* some of which were eventually collected in *All on the Irish Shore* in 1903. The editor of the *Badminton Magazine* now wrote to them asking them to write a series of such stories for him:

Therefore we sat out on the sand hills, roasting in the great sunshine of Northern France, and talked, until we had talked Major Sinclair Yeates, R.M., and Flurry Knox into existence. "Great Uncle MacCarthy's" Ghost and the adventure of the stolen foxes followed, as it were, of necessity. It has always seemed to us that character presupposes incident. The first thing needful is to know your man. Before we had left Étaples, we had learned to know most of the people of the R.M.'s country very well indeed, and all the better for the fact that, of them all, "Slipper" and "Maria" alone had prototypes in the world as we knew it.
—Ch. XXII, *Irish Memories*

They returned to Drishane in the autumn, having completed three of the stories. There now occurred an incident which was to have far-reaching consequences. On the first day of November, while out hunting, Martin was heavily thrown from her horse, "Dervish," which then completed the disaster by rolling on her. She was severely injured and was confined to bed for several months, scarcely able to move. The injury to her spine caused her severe pain for a long time after and this bad fall really seems to have begun the long, physical decline which ended in her death in 1915. However, they pressed on with the stories for the *Badminton,* working hard until the middle of the following year. The stories appeared at monthly intervals, from October 1898 to September 1899:

The twelve "R.M." stories kept us desperately at work until the beginning of August, 1899. Looking back on the writing of them, each one, as we finished it, seemed to be the last possible effort of exhausted nature. Martin hardly knew, through those strenuous months, what it was to be out of suffering. Even though it cannot be denied that we both of us found enjoyment in the writing of them, I look

back upon the finish of each story as a nightmare effort.
Copying our unspeakably tortuous Ms. till the small hours
of the morning of the last possible day; whirling through
the work of the illustrations. . . . By the time the last
bundle had been dispatched Martin and I had arrived
at a stage when we regarded an ink-bottle as a mad dog
does a bucket of water. Rest, and change of air, for both
of us, was indicated. I was sent to Aix, she went to North
Wales, and we decided to meet in Paris and spend the
winter there.

In the beginning of October, 1899, we established our-
selves in an *appartement* in the Boulevard Edgar Quinet,
and there we spent the next four months.
　　　　　　　　　　　—Ch. XXIII, *Irish Memories.*

It was in November, while they were in Paris, that Longmans published the first volume of the "R.M." stories
under the title *Some Experiences of an Irish R.M.* The
book was a huge success and brought them international
fame. The first edition of three thousand copies sold out
in a month and a second edition was called for. The first
dozen of the "R.M." stories brought the cousins the sort
of general acclaim which even their finest novel, published five years earlier, had not earned them.

In the "R.M." stories, Edith and Martin suspend
their awareness of the historical inevitabilities which
attend their class and present us with a comic universe
seen with the eye of love. Their earlier work, as has
been indicated, had given ample evidence of a darker
vision, but in their most celebrated stories they flee
reality and take happy refuge in a world compounded
of outrageously funny accidents and extravagant Irish
talk. To the making of this comic universe they brought
their dual sense of the ridiculous and their marvellous

ear for Munster speech. All their lives they had moved between two Irelands and had talked with double tongue. From the day-to-day encounters of their two worlds and the rich ambiguities born of the clash of two languages they produced a whirl of farce and chatter which moves at its own exciting pace, according to its own laws or absence of them, scorning the drabness of literal representation and pausing not for sober judgements. To ask of their comic world that it conform to rules entirely irrelevant to it is mere folly. We do not visit the world of Jeeves and Bertie Wooster in search of profound social comment; we do not quarry in a Feydeau farce for the grim realities of the French middle-class. Nor should we approach the "R.M." stories as though they ought to be a repository of the truth about late-nineteenth-century Ireland. What we must bring to our enjoyment of them is our sense of the essential daftness of circumstance, our joy in linguistic nuance, our delight in things going wonderfully wrong, our tolerance of two and two's everlasting failure to make a symmetrically satisfactory four, in short, a sense of humour sharpened by experience.

The stories do not set out to be profound explorations of character or telling analyses of social or political structures. They are comedy of incident realized within a stiff convention. The extremes of the convention are provided by the "gentry" at the top and the locals and servants at the bottom. We accept this without protest for the purposes of the comedy, just as we accept the essential absurdity of the Bertie Wooster-Jeeves relationship as the basis of the idiotic events in which they become involved together, and, as with the Bertie-Jeeves relationship, a large part of the comedy lies in the frequency with which the master-servant relationship is reversed. As long as the convention works to embroil both master and servant in a mutual comic debacle, all is well. Uneasy moments in regard to the motivation of real characters, such as have sometimes occurred in the early novels, are avoided in a situation where character has, as it were, been arbitrarily frozen so that a whirl of funny happenings can be set in motion. Real uneasiness arises only in relation to the no-man's-land between the extremes: the territory occupied by the Flynns and the McRorys, nouveau-riche social climbers who try to cross the "boundery-line" that divides the elect from their social inferiors. In the stories in which these characters appear, as will be seen later, the writers' control over their material tends to waver somewhat.

The opening story, "Great Uncle McCarthy," is highly effective in introducing us to the *milieu* and to a whole range of the characters, while yet remaining a brisk, comic story in its own right. We enter into the R.M.'s new world with the R.M. himself newly arrived in Skebawn and hunting for a house. The fine note of pervasive paradox is struck from the very beginning when Major Yeates, though desperately anxious to escape from Mrs. Raverty's dreadful hotel into his new home, finds himself giving both the carpenter and the plumber seven days without the option of a fine. As though he has not suffered enough, he has as his landlord Florence McCarthy Knox, the celebrated Flurry who "looked like a stable boy among gentlemen, and

a gentleman among stableboys" and who appropriately
makes his first entrance on the stage when he comes to
sell his new tenant a horse. Flurry is, of course, one of
the great creations of the whole "R.M." series. He ap-
pears in most of the stories, sometimes as the manipula-
tor, sometimes as himself the butt. His clan of relatives
ranges from Sir Valentine Knox of Castle Knox down
to the auctioneer Knox known as "Larry the Liar." If
Major Yeates is, for the writers' purpose, the perfectly
conceived innocent abroad, Flurry is his perfect cice-
rone, a kind of quietly manic Man Friday who leads his
Crusoe by the nose into ever stranger scrapes. Philippa
broods over the story as an unseen wife-to-be. All the
horrors of the house combine to suggest the shock which
awaits her arrival since Philippa, unlike the Major, is
wholly English and, therefore, likely to find the logic
of Skebawn not to her taste. We await her arrival with
appalled glee. The superb climax in which Flurry is
made to look memorably silly by running his mother's
first cousin to ground in the attic, thereby uncovering
the McCarthy Gannons who have been secretly squat-
ting in the Major's house and shooting his foxes, splendidly synthesizes the themes of the series. It is altogether
appropriate that the amiable scavengers among whom
he is to live should quarter themselves on the Major
from the beginning and that his servants should be
complicatedly in league with them. The roguery of
Skebawn lies in wait for Major Yeates in the heart of
his own house. How right it is, also, that the hunt, which
is going to be so important a part of his life from now
on, should pursue its first quarry right into the very

house itself. All the themes and all the people and all the wickedly hilarious contrivances come to roost under the Major's roof for our splendid delectation, in this first, compendious story. Here is God's plenty, with the comfortable assurance of more to come.

Before Philippa arrives on the Skebawn scene as Mrs. Yeates, the Major must be involved with Miss Bobby Bennett for purposes of subsequent embarrassment. Miss Bobby is a kind of female equivalent of Flurry. She is attractive, vigorous in speech, a good rider, an adept at entrapping reluctant gallants like Major Yeates into such unmasculine attentions as pinning up her hair during a hunt, an incident he will not soon be allowed to forget. More and more, the major is involved in the chaotically hilarious doings of Skebawn—more and more he wonders what Philippa will make of it all when she arrives. It is a considerable relief that Philippa proves as susceptible as the Major himself to Skebawn's peculiar charms. She turns up in person halfway through the series and, in "Philippa's Fox-Hunt," proclaims herself one of the elect by accompanying the hunt on her bicycle. She becomes infected by the excitement of the chase and ends up at the centre of a demented climax involving old Mrs. Knox, the latter's brother-in-law to whom Mrs. Knox has not spoken in twenty years, and a gaggle of clergymen called to the scene by the excited Philippa. Philippa quickly wins her spurs.

Old Mrs. Knox of Aussolas is a splendidly comic embodiment of the endearing aspects of Anglo-Irish idiosyncrasy. She is elderly, tough, magnificently individualistic. She quotes Virgil to the Major, screams like a macaw at the servants, serves splendid salmon on cracked dishes, wears diamond rings while feeding her hens and presides regally at her tenants' dance in the course of which she hitches up her skirts to dance a jig with the redoubtable Flurry. She epitomizes a gay, hard-riding, high-living, extravagant class at which, in these stories, Edith and Martin cast an unusually indulgent eye.

The "R.M." stories are the comic obverse of novels like *The Real Charlotte* and *The Big House of Inver*. The backgrounds are the same—tea-parties and boating expeditions, hunting and dancing, picnics and sports-days, flirtations and matchmakings. Only the angle of vision is different. The amusing trip in Bernard Shute's yacht, *Eileen Oge,* which ends with the slaughter of Dr. Fahy's cockatoo, recalls the near-disaster which over-takes Roderick Lambert, Francie Fitzpatrick and Christopher Dysart in the ill-fated *Daphne.* Lady Knox sounds remarkably like the Lady Dysart of Bruff who bewails the superfluity of women in her party. It is the same world but, this time, sunny side up.

The best of the stories partake of the confidence and sureness of touch which inform the best of the novels. It is, as always, a world of masters and servants but one in which the roles are, more often than not, comically reversed. At times the humor arises out of the doings of "the gentry," the Major, Mrs. Knox, Flurry, Sally etc. At other times it arises out of the gentry's unsuccessful encounters with the locals, as in "The Holy Island," where Major Yeates and the other representatives of law and order are made to look silly by the machiavel-lian Mr. Canty. Major Yeates moves through the series as the perfect exponent of the Anglo-Irish experience, the Englishman in him outraged by the lunacies of his encounters, the Irishman in him warmly responding to it all, the magistrate lost in the man and his desperate efforts after official propriety scattered to the winds by his English wife's delighted laughter.

Special scorn is reserved, as always with these writers, for one species only, the uncomprehending English tourist, most memorably embodied in the unhappy Leigh Kelway of "Lisheen Races, Second-Hand." This beautifully constructed story reduces the smugness of the visiting Briton to shreds in a series of tightly controlled declensions. As we jolt with him through the countryside in a series of doomed journeys, fated never to reach the race-meeting and increasingly embroiled in the murkiness of Irish events and Irish speech, we rejoice in the uproarious overthrow of all his English simplicities. Never has race-meeting been so memorably unvisited, never has the English failure to understand the Irish been so completely and good-humouredly demonstrated. There lie behind the story both a wealth of technical expertise on the part of the writers and the controlled, colonial resentment of an entire class. Leigh Kelway, a sort of Miss Hope-Drummond in trousers, comes to Ireland to write up "the liquor question" and moves inexorably to the dreadful, country pub where Slipper delivers his celebrated description of the Lisheen Races and Driscoll's "death." His final undoing, as the outraged Lord Waterbury surveys him lying in the ruins of two coaches on the roadside, is a superbly contrived climax to a brilliantly managed narrative.

This first volume of "R.M." stories contains one of a tragic nature, "The Waters of Strife," a story written during the second half of the November in which Martin sustained her severe fall. It is fourth in the series and appeared in the January 1899 issue of the *Badminton Magazine*. A quarrel after a local regatta leads to a fight in which Bat Callaghan kills Jim Foley. The murderer disappears and the police, though they succeed in satisfying themselves of Callaghan's guilt, fail to find the murderer. Callaghan pays a mysterious midnight visit to Major Yeates's house to inform him of the whereabouts of his victim's corpse and Mrs. Callaghan, Bat's mother, solicits the Major's assistance to keep her out of court. Time passes and the affair is gradually forgotten. Later, Major Yeates is invited to a stag-party by his old regiment who wish to make him a presentation in honour of his forthcoming marriage. While he is a guest at the regiment's quarters, one of the sentries, an Irishman named Harris, shoots at a face which is staring at him from the top of a high wall. When the face continues to stare at him, Harris goes mad and shoots himself. Next morning Major Yeates recognizes "Harris" as Bat Callaghan, done to death by the ghost of his victim who has been conjured up by his guilty conscience.

The story is quite unlike anything else in this first volume of "R.M." stories in that it concerns itself seriously with a tragedy which takes place outside the secure world of the Major and Flurry and Mrs. Knox. No very profound exploration of this world, which is seen as one of violence and superstition, "The Waters of Strife" is nevertheless held together and given a certain validity by the economical and effectively pathetic depiction of Bat's mother, the Widow Callaghan. Her letter, found in the dead man's pocket, has a ring of accuracy about it reminiscent of Synge. This darker world, on the periphery of the jocund arena in which the majority of the "R.M." stories are played out, is allowed to intrude but rarely into the sunny center of things. In the second volume of "R.M." stories, the earlier part of "Oweneen the Sprat" shows the Major's comfortable world being intimidated by menace from the darker periphery, the Major himself being the culprit on this occasion. However, this later story is resolved in a comic exposure of the blackmailers and the Major's universe is restored to its customary serenity. Inside the laager, the common people appear as suppletongued servants, outside they are, usually, amiable adjuncts to the comedy but very occasionally, as in "The Waters of Strife," a discordant note intrudes. There is just enough of this darker mode to hint at the writers' awareness of the fragile unreality of the world of comedy they are spreading before us.

The first volume of the "R.M." stories ends in triumphant comedy with Flurry Knox's wedding to Sally Knox and the resolving of the dispute between old Mrs. Knox and Lady Knox. "Oh Love, Oh Fire!" is a merry mélange of dancing and devious dalliance which winds up the book on a suitable note of lovers' meetings at journey's end. This last story appeared in the *Badminton Magazine* in September 1899, and a mere two months later the series was put into book form by Longmans. The speed with which they moved to publication is a tribute to the popularity of the stories as they appeared and to the publishers' conviction that the series made a satisfactory unit. As invariably happens with such sets of stories, a few, while functioning adequately within the group, work less well on their own account. One recalls how this occurs even in Joyce's *Dubliners,* where "After the Race" is clearly a thinner story than many of the others, one which more requires the support given to it by its context in the group of which it is part. Similarly, in the first "R.M." book, "The Policy of the Closed Door," while furthering the courtship of Flurry and Sally Knox, does little else of real interest or value. Because it is so dependent on its setting in the series as a whole, it is less artistically autonomous than many of the other stories.

Major Yeates is the key to the book's success. He is the perfect guide to the world we explore with him, the most genial and likeable of hosts. Maurice Collis, in a felicitously Anglo-Irish lapse, surely caused by a nudge from Slipper's ghost, tells us that "Major Yeates is partially of Irish abstraction, but the Irish scene is quite new to him." Yes, indeed! Later on, of course, when the Irish scene is no longer quite so new to him, the major is rather less "abstracted" but he remains at all times entirely "partial." It is his partiality which woos and wins us.

Nine years were to elapse between the first and second books of "R.M." stories. During that time, as might be expected, the collaborators' literary agent, J. B. Pinker, frequently urged the cousins to create a second

volume while the vogue lasted. However, they were
both busy in their separate ways and the work simply
did not get done for a long time. Edith, whose father
had died in 1898, was now head of the household at
Drishane and constantly busy with the running of the
farm and the house. In 1903 she also undertook fresh
responsibilities as Master of the West Carbery Hunt.
Violet's health was uncertain and she had to spend some
time at health spas in such places as Buxton (whither
old Mrs. Knox was to be fictionally dispatched in later
"R.M." stories) . However, as a stopgap, they agreed to
collect some of their hunting stories, which had appeared in various magazines, and in 1903 these appeared
under the title *All on the Irish Shore*. These are, in
the main, hunting or horsey stories with a light love interest and are, generally, much inferior to the "R.M."
stories. The humor is often of a clumsily facetious kind
with periphrastic contrivance taking the place of good
plots. In "A Grand Filly," a story written by Edith alone
and originally published in the *Badminton Magazine*
of April 1897, the figure of Miss Trinder is clearly an
early sketch of old Mrs. Knox of Aussolas. Another of
the stories, "An Irish Problem," is interesting in that it
shows the writers exploring the comic possibilities of a
scene familiar in Anglo-Irish fiction generally, the court-
room encounter in which an interpreter is needed for
an Irish-speaking litigant and the comedy arises from
the ensuing linguistic mêlée. This is amusingly done
and recalls similar scenes in such novels as *The Col-
legians* and *The Rivals* by Gerald Griffin.

The book sold well and Longmans pressed the writers

for further work of the same kind. As the second volume of "R.M." stories was still incomplete, they put together, at Longman's request, a collection of articles and occasional pieces. These appeared in 1906 under the title *Some Irish Yesterdays*. Violet referred to this as "the rubbish book" but Longmans paid them £150 and excellent royalties for it all the same. Pinker continued to press them for a further "R.M." book and, finally, in the autumn of 1908, *Further Experiences of an Irish R.M.* was published by Longmans and sold extremely well, new editions being constantly called for.

In this second series, Major Yeates is rather less the neophyte than he has previously been. In fact, we learn in the opening story, "The Pug-Nosed Fox," that he is actually deputy M.F.H. in place of Flurry Knox, during the latter's absence with the Irish Yeomanry at the South African War. The Major is still wax in the hands of the locals but he scores over Flurry on quite a number of occasions, notably in the concluding story, "The Whiteboys," where he is allowed to triumph in Flurry's special, canine province. The Major is now the proud but harassed father of two rather pestilential boys who are given to taking fright at the slightest strange incident, a habit which would seem to render them peculiarly unfitted for the hectic universe they are called upon to inhabit. Children are not the *forte* of these writers, any more than passionate love scenes.

One of the finest of the "R.M." stories is "Poisson D'Avril," in which the Major, on his way to a family wedding at the English home of their relative, Alice Hervey, undergoes a series of hilarious adventures in improbable trains and crowded country hotels. Edith and Martin, who spent a good deal of time on various temperamental Irish trains, are particularly amusing when they describe the vicissitudes of rail travel. The cheerless waiting rooms where the fires smoke but do not burn, the unexplained halts at unidentified spots on the line, the angry English travellers who find it all quite intolerable, the highly individuaiistic railway officials who are prepared to advise passengers on the buying of salmon but profess to know nothing about timetables—over it all broods what the story calls "the inveterate supremacy in Ireland of the personal element." Inevitably, the Major misses his connection with the Mail Train and finds himself stranded at Loughranny. The town is thronged for an Irish festival of music and dance and Major Yeates is lucky to get a bed on a palliasse under the billiard-table in the local hotel. His early-morning encounter with the First Prize for Reels, who has spent the night on top of the billiard table and whose feet are "like three-pound loaves with the dint of the little dancing-shoes I had on me in the competition last night," is entirely a delight. His eventual arrival at Alice Hervey's very English home with quite the wrong sort of parcel provides one of the best climaxes in the series. As in "Lisheen Races, Second Hand," this story of another comic journey is beautifully constructed with a fine balance of comic incident and dialogue. There is no straining after effect, no uneasiness in the handling of the characters. The Major is at his most endearing as he struggles with his perennial task of reconciling the demands of his two universes and comes inevitably to grief. Another equally effective

story is "The Last Day of Shraft." In this, the Major
finds himself burdened with a troublesome visitor in
the shape of Philippa's elderly stepbrother, Maxwell
Bruce, who is an Irish-language and folklore enthusiast.
The series of misadventures by which the Major, local
representative of law and order, and his serious-minded
brother-in-law find themselves warmly entrapped in
Mrs. Brickley's shebeen in a fume of illicit whiskey and
old Irish song is delightfully contrived. The humor is
worthy of a Flann O'Brien.

Much less happy are the effects achieved in the story
"Sharper Than a Ferret's Tooth," in which we once
again encounter the McRory family, whom we have previously met in "The Pug-Nosed Fox." The McRorys
are cheerful parvenus who have been socially accepted
(after a struggle) because the sons are handsome, the
daughters pretty and cheerful and the mother good-
humoredly prepared to buy generously at local bazaars.
In the clumsily-titled "Sharper Than a Ferret's Tooth,"
Philippa and Miss Shute are trying to marry off Bernard
Shute to the Major's niece, Sybil Hervey. Sybil is, unfortunately, more interested in the handsome Curly
McRory. As a result of a minor mishap in a boat, the
Major's entire party finds itself stranded in the McRory
house, dripping wet, in need of clothes and hot food
and drink. All these things are provided instantly by the
open-handed McRorys who entertain the whole party
royally. The snag is that Sybil is thrown into Curly's
willing arms, thus frustrating Philippa's and Miss
Shute's matchmaking plans for Bernard. The situation
is an anticipation, on the comic level, of aspects of
Edith's later novel, *Mount Music.* In fact, Mrs. Mc-

Rory is clearly the prototype of Mrs. Mangan in the later work. It would seem to be the writers' aim to depict the McRorys (as Edith later depicts the Mangans) as cheerful vulgarians. The trouble is that it is the "gentry" group whose vulgarity is here most clearly exposed. The McRorys' only sin is that they rescue the dripping voyagers, clothe them, feed them, entertain them and captivate the "lady" intended for Bernard Shute. The complacent vulgarity of the "gentry" group is exposed in a fashion which can hardly, one feels, have been the writers' intention. Philippa, Sally Knox and Miss Shute jeer at Mrs. McRory's taste in clothes and sneer when they are offered "a choice of about eighty silk blouses." Even the Major is allowed a mild sneer at the immaculate "Lounge Suit" lent to him by the handsome Curly. The elaborate meal offered by the McRorys is made the subject of further mockery: the food is of the wrong kind, wrongly served and there is too much of it anyhow. The whole point is that "real gentry" can afford to do without this kind of crude excess, that money is no substitute for blood. Unfortunately, bad manners are no substitute for courtesy. The writers, on this occasion, actually make us dislike the Major's family group and their associates, a bad error which conflicts with the whole nature of the series and shatters the convention within which they are working. The comedy of situation at which they excel has momentarily broken down and something unpleasant from the real world has briefly intruded. On the whole, Edith was to handle such complications more tolerantly and more acceptably in her later novels.

5

End of a Partnership:
Dan Russel the Fox *(1911) and*
In Mr Knox's Country *(1915)*

The seven years between the publication of the second volume of "R.M." stories and the death of Violet Martin produced only two further works of any importance, the rather lightweight novel, *Dan Russel the Fox,* in 1911 and the third and final volume of the "R.M." stories published in the year of Martin's death, 1915, under the title *In Mr Knox's Country.* It is matter for genuine regret that the partners had not, with the creative confidence engendered in them by *The Real Charlotte,* moved on from that fine novel to even greater fictional heights. Their failure to do so may be explained in various ways. Pinker, who had become their literary agent in 1896, and Longmans, pleased by the success of the "R.M." stories, constantly pressed them to produce more work of that nature and the cousins' need for money forced them to comply with this request instead of devoting to their fictions the slow and careful preparation which had gone to the making of *The Real Charlotte*. Martin's health, never robust, declined after her serious hunting accident and she required various rest cures from time to time, both in Ireland and abroad. Edith was busily occupied with the running of the house and farm at "Drishane," where she and her younger sister, Hildegarde, had started a dairy farm with twenty-five Friesian cows, the first of their breed to be imported into Ireland. This enterprising venture failed, however, and the herd had to be sold at a loss in 1911. Edith had taken over the Mastership of the West Carbery Hunt from her brother, Aylmer, in 1903 and, though she relinquished it in 1909, she resumed it again a few years later when she had been relieved of the cares of the dairy farm. In spite of domestic cares and illnesses (and, indeed, sometimes *because* of these latter) the cousins travelled a good deal in these years, together and separately. Early in 1910 they were both honored guests at a banquet for Irish women writers given by a Dublin body known as The Corinthian Dinner Committee. In the same year they visited Pinker at his home in Surrey and went on to stay with Edith's brother, Cameron, at Kneller Hall in Twickenham. Later in that year, Edith was once again in England, this time to attend the wedding of her younger brother, Jack, in London. In June 1911, Martin went to London with a large family party to attend the coronation of George V and in September of that year she and Edith visited Annecy and other places on the Lac d'Annecy. At this period also, both women were actively involved in the affairs of the Munster Women's Franchise League, an organization of suffragettes of which Edith was president and Martin a vice-president.

Dan Russel the Fox had been begun as early as 1904, while the writers were at Amélie-les-Bains in the interests of Martin's health; but they had abandoned the novel after a few chapters and did not resume it until 1909 when they were at Portofino with Hildegarde and a friend, Miss Nora Tracey. It is a longer novel than *The Silver Fox* and handles the same themes in a more straightforward manner, omitting the element of fantasy. Wealthy, young English heiress, Katherine Rowan, on holiday at Aix-les-Bains with a friend, Mrs. Masterman, has an encounter with a dapper and engaging little Irishwoman, Mrs. Delanty, as a result of which she comes to Ireland for an extended stay. The visit turns into the usual process of discovery of the strange land. Katherine becomes a devotee of the hunt and the book broadens into a series of hunting scenes which are portrayed with great vigor. Katherine, having fallen in love with the hunt, now proceeds to make the mistake of falling in love also with the huntsman, one John Michael Fitz-Symons, younger brother of the Master of the Hunt. John Michael is handsome and inarticulate and Katherine's involvement with him infuriates her other suitor, a writer named Ulick Adare. Adare proposes to Katherine, in a scene where the girl's embarrassment seems to reflect the authors' inability to handle such passages:

> "You might be as rude to me as you liked; it would be better than torture." The last word was almost inaudible. Katherine took a step backwards, so sudden was the

shock, and so strangely mixed with it the instinct to get
away from him.

"That's putting it rather strongly," she said, red to the
roots of her hair, but still trying hard to be commonplace.

Mrs. Delanty, the neat, capable little Irishwoman re-
sponsible for attracting Katherine to Ireland, is, however, a successful creation and her gulling of the silly
Fanshawe is amusingly handled. John Michael, a combination of sex appeal and stupidity, is a sort of inarticulate Mellors who insists on confining his atten-
tion to game-keeping (or, in John Michael's case, to
hounds). The writers' inability to follow through to
any kind of logical conclusion the consequences of
Katherine's sexual interest in the unresponsive John
Michael produces a number of awkward scenes, culmi-
nating in a tortuously contrived climax at the Fitz-
Symons' house. Mrs. Fitz-Symons urges her stolid son
to propose marriage to Katherine and he recoils in
horror from the suggestion, loudly asserting that he
would "sooner sweep a kennel in America" than offer
himself in marriage to the lady. Katherine overhears his
unflattering protestations and is abruptly restored by
the shock to the safety of the bosom of her own class.
As the novel closes, she is back once more on the con-
tinent, convalescing safely at Portofino, and Ulick Adare
is about to sail into her life once again:

> As for Ireland, Ireland was a tradition, a grey spot astray
> upon a misty ocean. In a remote past things had hap-
> pened there; she thought of them as little as possible, but
> sometimes they sprang upon her unawares, and made her
> understand that we may regret our sins, but we agonize
> over our follies.

The progress of the novel, lively enough at times, is badly flawed by the writers' unwillingness to pursue the implications of the sexual motifs they sound. Even when Mrs. Delanty, who is no English lady but merely a vulgar and calculating little Irish nobody with a good figure, offers herself to the incredible John Michael, reluctance is the response of the writers as well as the swain:

> "Johnny!" she cried, beginning to sob, "wouldn't you stay for my sake? Don't you know how fond I am of you?"
>
> What more she said neither she nor John Michael can ever clearly remember, nor do they desire to do so, but in that insane moment of surrender and self-forgetfulness, the small, second-rate, egotistical soul of Mrs. Delanty found wings, and spread them in a larger air.
>
> It was over in an instant, and she knew that she had given herself away for nothing. They were standing opposite each other in suffocating tension and embarrassment.

Mrs. Delanty is forced to console herself by marrying the equally egregious but conveniently infatuated Fanshawe.

In a sense, we are unhappily back once more with the grosser simplicities of some of the earlier fiction. English heiresses do not marry Irish huntsmen, and if they are indiscreet enough to lust after them then they must be shepherded away to safer places, however gauche the contrivance which ensures their deliverance. Violet Powell describes the novel as "well-constructed" but many of the characters are mere stereotypes. In *Dan Russel the Fox* the "R.M." world is being uneasily used for the exploration of character and motive. The weakness of the novel is caused by a clash of conventions

and the writers' unwillingness or inability to write
frankly about sex.

In 1913, the writers' relationship with Longmans was
poisoned by an episode which caused them considerable
anger and distress. In that year, Longmans published a
collection of "Stories of Irish Life and Sport" by "Owen
Roe & Honor Urse." The title of this troublesome book
was *By the Brown Bog* and it was an evident pastiche
of the "R.M." stories. Longmans even included at the
front of the book an advertisement for the works of
Somerville and Ross. Edith and Martin reacted vigor-
ously to the situation and called in the assistance of both
Pinker and the Society of Authors. After a lengthy
wrangle, Longmans agreed to remove from the collection the first story, the one which bore the closest re-
semblance to the "R.M." stories. This was entitled
"The Worsting of Head Constable McKeever" and in
it, as Edith was quick to demonstrate, whole passages
had been lifted from the "R.M." stories, with clumsy
changes here and there.

The year 1915, which was to rob Edith of her collaborator, saw the publication of the third and final
volume of "R.M." stories. Shortly afterwards, in *Irish
Memories,* she described the circumstances in which
this volume came into being:

> I suppose it was the result of old habit, and of the return
> of the hounds, but, for whatever reason, during the years
> that followed the appearance of "Dan Russel the Fox",
> Martin and I put aside the notions we had been dwelling
> upon in connection with "a serious novel," and took to
> writing "R.M." stories again. These, six couple of them
> (like the first draft of the re-established pack), wandered

through various periodicals, chiefly *Blackwood's Magazine,* and, in July, 1915, they were published in a volume with the title of "In Mr Knox's Country".

One of the stories in this collection, "When I First Met Dr Hickey," harks back, as its title suggests, to the early days of Major Yeates's stay in Ireland. When Edith later edited a full collection of the "R.M." stories she placed this one immediately after the opening story, "Great Uncle McCarthy." It is a pleasant story, which moves at a brisk pace and has a suitably uproarious climax. In general, however, the stories in this last volume depict both an ageing major and an ageing Ireland. The Major and Flurry Knox are greying and the large estates have passed, through a series of Land Acts, out of the possession of the gentry. In "The Finger of Mrs Knox" the mood is mordantly nostalgic. The Major and Mrs. Knox sit by the fire in the hall of Aussolas Castle, reminiscing about the past and are visited by Stephen Casey, the son of one of Mrs. Knox's former tenants. Casey is in the clutches of Goggin, a local "gombeen," a figure similar to Jeremiah Donovan of *Naboth's Vineyard.* Unable to pay his debt to Goggin, Stephen Casey runs the risk of having his cattle seized in settlement of his debt and appeals to Mrs. Knox for assistance. Her bitter reply reveals the change in the times:

> "I have no tenants," replied Mrs. Knox tartly; "the Government is your landlord now, and I wish you joy of each other!"

With suitably touching loyalty, Casey protests his preference for the old paternalistic order of things and is sent round to the servants' hall for his tea, while the lady of the manor broods over his problem. In the event, she prevails against Goggin on Casey's behalf and the stark issues of the situation are dissolved in a comic hunting debacle, with the Major acting as a convenient catalyst. In spite of the comedy, however, there is no mistaking the presence of a sunset touch. The old days are gone for ever and a new and less congenial order is taking the place of the hereditary ascendancy.

Not all the stories carry these ominous overtones. "The Bosom of the McRorys" and "The Comte de Pralines" are cheerful romps in the series' most relaxed manner. In "The Friend of Her Youth" the central figure of Chichester recalls the unfortunate Leigh Kelway of "Lisheen Races, Second Hand." He is "an elderly young man, worn smooth by much visiting in country houses" and he is made to come to grief among a hearty yachting set, a milieu which recalls parts of *The Real Charlotte* and of earlier "R.M." stories. Altogether, this last collection of "R.M." stories, though intermittently very funny, has it in both overtones of bitterness and a strong sense of *déjà-vu*. The writers fall back on situations often exploited before and there is not, in this book, any sense of a coherent chronological progress such as governs the other two in the series.

In August 1915, Edith and Martin set out for what was to prove their last holiday together. This took them to Kerry and, later, in *Wheel-Tracks* (1924), Edith was to recall the holiday with intense and painful delight and to assert that "did Yesterday indeed come again, it would be from among those yesterdays that I would choose my day." After their return from Kerry to "Drishane," Martin began to feel unwell, complaining of pains in the face and head. Through the months of September and October various diagnoses were hazarded. Her eyes were examined and she had two teeth removed but no cure was effected and, late in November, her doctor, O'Meara, advised her to enter the "Glen Vera" Nursing Home in Cork for observation and treatment. In early December, she became unconscious and a tumour was located at the base of the brain and declared inoperable. Edith was told to send for Jim Martin, Violet's nearest relative, who was then in Galway. Throughout the month of December, Edith watched and waited helplessly for the end, sitting by the bedside, holding Martin's cold hand in hers and looking in anguish on the face of her companion, who no longer recognized her or gave any sign. On 18 December, Edith began a chalk drawing of her dying cousin which shows Martin withdrawn into the trance of imminent death. The end came three days later, on 21 December. Martin's body was taken to Castle Townshend the following day and the coffin placed in the church of St. Barrahane which stands high above the harbor of the little town. She was buried in the churchyard of St. Barrahane on the 23 December. Edith, broken by grief and unable to believe that "the incredible impossible" was happening, could not bear to attend the interment. The unbroken and devoted partnership of three decades, which had produced over a dozen books, was now at an end and Edith, crushed by her grief, believed she would write no more.

6

Reminiscence and Renewal:
Irish Memories (1917),
Mount Music (1919) *and*
An Enthusiast (1921)

For some time before Martin's death, Edith, and indeed their entire Castle Townshend circle, had been cultivating an active interest in spiritualism. She was encouraged in this interest by an amateur medium named Jem Barlow who had come to stay at "Drishane" in 1912 and later rented a house in the village. In the summer of the year following Martin's death, while Edith and Jem Barlow were experimenting with attempts at automatic script, they recorded messages which, Edith came to believe, emanated from Martin. These messages indicated that their literary partnership had only been interrupted, not terminated, and that their work together would continue. Overjoyed at the possibility of reestablishing some link with her adored cousin, Edith joined Jem Barlow in further sessions of automatic writing and came to believe quite firmly that she was in communication with the spirit of the dead woman. It was in this conviction that she appended to all her subsequent works, apart from a few minor pieces to which the belief was not relevant, the dual signature which had appeared on all the work hitherto produced together by "Somerville and Ross."

The first concrete result of Edith's renewal was the volume, *Irish Memories,* published late in 1917. This is a collection of reminiscences which takes its beginning from Violet Martin and centers largely around her but occasionally divagates into accounts of various Somerville family figures and family doings, with pieces of older, historical reminiscence thrown in here and there. It is a discursive work which will prove irritating to the methodically minded but it is held together by the genuine warmth which infuses the comment on Violet Martin and the book remains a useful storehouse of information on the early doings of the two writers. Violet's own unfinished memoir of her brother, Robert Martin, forms the opening chapter. The book was favorably reviewed and Edith, encouraged by her spiritualistic "contacts" with Martin and often drawing on her memories of projects they had discussed while Martin was still alive, went back to her work as a writer. She had over thirty years of life before her and was to produce five more full-length novels, at least two of them of major proportions. In addition, she was to achieve over ten other works varying from travel books to reminiscent sketches and family biography.

Mount Music (1919), says Edith in a short Preface, "was planned some years ago by Martin Ross and myself. A few portions of it were written, and it was then put aside for other work."

It is easy to guess why the partners may have found it difficult to proceed with the book at the time of its first devising. The theme of the novel is intermarriage between Catholic and Protestant at Big-House level and requires the exploration of sensitive areas of experience and behavior which were largely closed to these writers. The only novel in which they had previously attempted insight into the world of the Catholic Irish, *Naboth's Vineyard* (1891), had proved, at best, an honorable failure. They had always functioned most effectively, on both serious and humorous levels, as explorers of their own, Protestant, Ascendancy universe. However, since they saw the rise of a Catholic middle-class as part of the social assault which was to undermine the Protestant Ascendancy's dominance, it was inevitable that they would have to progress to some attempt at depicting and analyzing the resultant conflict. On a comic level, the McRory family represents a rather unsuccessful attempt to introduce a well-to-do Catholic family into the highly stylized world of the "R.M." stories. As has already been suggested, the results were not always happy. It is, of course, nowhere explicitly stated that the McRorys are Catholics but, at the beginning of "The Bosom of the McRorys," one of the longer stories from *In Mr Knox's Country,* it is clearly suggested that they are:

There befell a Harvest Festival in Skebawn Church, with a Bishop, and an Anthem, and a special collection. To it the McRorys, forsaking their own place of worship, came in power. . . .   ..

This, in itself, is hardly convincing, since it is most unlikely that even a wealthy Catholic family would attend service at a Protestant Church in a small village in the Ireland of the turn of the century.

In "The Bosom of the McRorys," of course, the religious issue is of no significance and the detail, however improbable, does not interfere with the subsequent comedy which is, as always, a flurry of incident. In *Mount Music,* however, Edith tackles the religious issue head-on and makes it the central theme of a long and serious novel. The family at the center of the novel is that of Major Richard Talbot-Lowry of Mount Music, an ageing, handsome, Anglo-Irish squire who has married, rather late in life, an Englishwoman a good deal younger and wealthier than himself. The estate adjoining Mount Music, Coppinger's Court, has descended to young Larry Coppinger, the son of Richard Talbot-Lowry's first-cousin. Larry's mother, an English Catholic of good family, has died but not before prevailing on her husband to become a Catholic. Larry's father dies also, leaving Larry to be brought up at Coppinger Court by his rigidly Protestant Aunt Frederica. She feels it her duty to obey, whatever her own misgivings, the dying wishes of the boy's parents and, so, Larry, heir to the desirable property of Coppinger Court and second cousin of the young Talbot-Lowrys, is brought up as a Catholic in a society where Catholicism is normally the religion of the servants and laborers.

This situation is presented by Edith with a good deal of quiet irony at the expense of the Protestant Ascendancy group.

The opening of the novel is, perhaps, self-indulgently circuitous, in a manner of which Martin might have been rather impatient, but the leisurely pace does allow the writer to set out the emergent issues of the novel with a good deal of quiet humor and a great deal of geniality. The scene, in Chapter IV, where Aunt Frederica and the Major discuss the awkwardness of the situation created by Larry's Catholicism, is a dexterously handled exercise in quiet satire. Edith may not at any stage penetrate very profoundly into the Catholic mind but she does manage to view her own Protestant Ascendancy clique with a good deal of detachment and humorous understanding.

As early as the opening of Chapter II, she indicates her awareness of the ambiguous relationship between the two halves of the society she is observing:

> In the days when Christian Talbot-Lowry was a little girl, that is to say between the eighties and nineties of the nineteenth century, the class known as Landed Gentry was still pre-eminent in Ireland. Tenants and tradesmen bowed down before them, with love sometimes, sometimes with hatred, never with indifference. The newspapers of their districts recorded their enterprises in marriage, in birth, in death, copiously, and with a servile rapture of detail . . .

This kind of passage speaks from within the Ascendancy laager, indicating the clique's sensitivity to hostile currents from without and its profound consciousness of the special position in which it stood in relation to the mass of the people. Edith also feels it necessary to indicate early on her purposeful fairness of approach:

> . . . one assurance, at least, may be offered without reservation. Those differing Paths, that alike have led many wayfarers to the rest that is promised to the Saints, will be treated with an equal reverence and respect.

Ideally, one would have wished this objectivity of approach to have been demonstrated in the fabric of the novel itself instead of being set out at the beginning as part of the writer's programme, but Edith is here writing for the first time by herself a full-length novel on a theme from which she and her partner had earlier shied away. It is not surprising that a task which had daunted their joint talents should prove a strain on the surviving partner's skill.

The central action of the novel concerns the love-affair between young Larry Coppinger and Christian Talbot-Lowry, the Major's favorite daughter. The complications in the plot are brought about by the figure who constitutes the book's principal achievement in characterization, big Dr. Mangan, the local G.P. who is a well-to-do Catholic possessed of a thriving practice, an amiable spouse and an attractive daughter, Tishy, whom he can place in Larry's way as a rival to Christian. Dr. Mangan schemes to get Major Richard Talbot-Lowry into his clutches by lending him money until he himself eventually becomes the real owner of Mount Music. When all his schemes have almost come to fruition, Dr Mangan is drowned in a flood while answering a sick call and old Evans, the butler from Mount Music who has, throughout, been made the spokesman for bigoted intolerance, stands over his body and speaks his bitter epitaph:

> "Well, ye wanted Mount Music!" he said, at last. "How d'ye like it now ye've got it?"

Edith brings to the depiction of Dr. Mangan considerable sympathy and force. He is a schemer and a social climber but he is big and generous in heart and he presents a striking contrast to his weakling victim, Major Dick. When he has died, the book offers him, in addition to Evans's bigoted bitterness, a paragraph of warmly human approval concluding with the words:

> He had lived according to the light he had received, and in his last act he took his life in his hand and gave it for another.

Dr. Mangan, then, though a threat to the safety of the Ascendancy group in the novel, wins the writer's warm approval for his positive qualities of courage, family feeling and dynamic energy. He is defeated by an accident, not for want of the will to shape circumstances to his own liking. Major Richard Talbot-Lowry, on the other hand, is a poor specimen of his type. Edith dubs his class "the Plesiosauridae or Pterodactyli," indicating that they are survivals who have outlived their age. Richard Talbot-Lowry is the supreme example of the species, and when ruin descends upon him he can do nothing to cope with his situation. He and his wife simply run away. When Dr. Mangan, through a firm of solicitors, forecloses on the Mount Music property,

Major Dick's reactions are described in heavily scornful tones:

> Dick Talbot-Lowry received this announcement with the mixture of indignation and contempt that might have been anticipated from an old-established Pterodactyl, who has been warned that his hereditary wallow in the Primeval Ooze is about to be wrested from him.

The Talbot-Lowrys' departure from their "hereditary wallow" is not sentimentalized or glamorized. This is an inept retreat in bad order and the novel treats it ruthlessly as such:

> On Monday morning Christian saw her father and mother start, too agitated by their coming journey to have a spare thought for sentiment; too much beset by the fear of what they might lose, their keys, their sandwiches, their dressing-boxes, to shed a tear for what they were losing, and had lost.

The technique of the novel is noticeably slacker than that of the writers' best work but it is a book in which a great deal of intelligent detachment combines with an honestly acknowledged involvement to produce a convincing generosity of outlook. Edith seems to acknowledge her inability to bring the work to an entirely satisfactory conclusion and settles for summarily marrying Larry to Christian once Dr. Mangan is dead and his daughter has run off with another suitor. "Summaries are tedious, and demand a skill, in making them endurable, that is bestowed on few" she concludes. The difficult material has proved ultimately intractable and the writer settles, as she and her partner had long ago done

in *Naboth's Vineyard,* for a melodramatic climax to un-
manageable events. The book's strength lies in the hon-
est attempt made at bridging the sectarian gap. To ap-
preciate the extent of the advance this represents, one
has only to put the ineffable McRorys side by side with
the Mangans. Equally, one might contrast the effete
Talbot-Lowrys with the robust, hard-jumping squires
of the "R.M." world to realize the extent to which Edith
had constituted herself a judge and critic of her own set.

The publication of *Mount Music* was followed a year
later by a volume of assorted pieces collected under the
title *Strayaways* (1920). The peculiar interest of this
volume is that it includes a number of Violet Martin's
own writings and provides, therefore, an opportunity
for studying the separate characteristics of her style. The
bulk of the volume is Martin's. It includes what Edith
describes as "Martin Ross's two earliest essays": "A Dele-
gate of the National League" and "Cheops in Connemara." The longest single item in the book is "In the
State of Denmark," the account of their 1893 tour,
which has been discussed already. "At the River's Edge"
and "Two Sunday Afternoons" are examples of Martin's work in the genre of the serious short story, both
showing more willingness to linger over the analysis
of passion than is elsewhere exhibited in the joint work
of these writers. "At the River's Edge" is a pensive and
lyrical piece, rather suggesting some of the early stories
of Sean O'Faolain. "Two Sunday Afternoons" is a realistic and violent story of terrorist violence and intrigue.
Not so tightly organized as it might be, it is nevertheless
an impressive piece of work which brings to us the very

flavor of the servant girl's crude and simple life and the pointless horror of her death, when she is caught up in the political hatreds of her day. It was these murky political passions which Edith tried to explore in her next novel, a shorter and slighter work than *Mount Music*.

An Enthusiast (1921) has as its background the troubled times through which Edith and the rest of her West Cork acquaintances were living, the period "of burning police barracks and Irishmen murdered by their brothers," the time of the Black-and-Tans, of raid and counter-raid. The "enthusiast" of the title is Dan Palliser, a young man of good family who naively hopes to solve Ireland's problems by economic means, by improved farming methods, by the introduction of properly run creameries and cooperative societies. He inevitably comes to grief, caught between the opposing antagonisms and suspicions of his own class and the local farmers. The former mistrust him because of his friendly relations with people suspected of Republican sympathies, the latter because of his Ascendancy origins. The novel begins and ends appropriately with death. As it opens, Dan's father's coffin is standing at the door of Monalour House, draped in the Union Jack, with the old Colonel's shining, brass-scabbarded sword lying on top. As it closes, Dan himself lies dead outside the house with the old Crimean sword in his hand, shot to death by one of his own house guests during an arms raid by Republicans on the family home. Appropriately, he lies between the two forces which have brought about his ruin, clutching an antiquated weapon which is itself a suitable symbol of the way time and events have passed him by.

The novel works well in its depiction of local, small-town politics. There is a splendidly amusing exposé of petty machinations at Rural District Council level. Mr. "Baby Bullet" Coyne is a delightful comic creation. Equally, the intolerances of the local squirearchy are once again, as in *Mount Music,* dispassionately observed. Edith manages to convey something of the turbulence of the period as it must have looked to a well-disposed member of the old order which was about to be displaced. She tries valiantly to intensify the novel's interest by introducing a hopeless love-affair between Dan Palliser and the wife of his tenant, Colonel Ducarrig, but this part of the novel is much less satisfactory than the efficient account given of small-town rivalries and Big House obscurantism. *An Enthusiast* is, at best, competent work without much really deep penetration of character or motive. Edith is setting up oppositions between groups rather than exploring individual psyches.

7

The Later Fiction: The Big House of Inver *(1925)*, French Leave *(1928)* and Sarah's Youth *(1938)*

Edith spent the troubled years during which the new Irish Free State was brought to the birth at Drishane House. She had petitioned for the pardoning of the condemned insurrectionaries of 1916 and later described herself as "half rebel and Miss-Facing-both-ways." She was witnessing the passing away of the administrative power of her own class and she was to live through the dreadful period of the Civil War in one of the most troubled corners of Ireland. The battle between Republicans and Free Staters was at its fiercest in West Cork and the Big Houses of the old ruling class were an obvious target for ancient resentments. However, the Somerville family was highly regarded by all in the locality and Drishane was to come through the troubles safely, only occasionally robbed of a horse or two by visiting marauders. Edith, though pressed by her friend Ethel Smyth to flee to England, stayed at Drishane through all the violence, trying to take her mind off current events by writing and painting when she could. In 1923, after the Civil War had ended, she published *Wheel-Tracks*, another "store of memories" concerning Drishane and the Irish world which had now passed away. Edith visited London during this year and Longmans advanced her £400 for *Wheel-Tracks*. During this visit, she also exhibited her paintings at Walker's Galleries in Bond Street and made a profit of £230. She returned to Drishane for Christmas, 1923. During 1924 she set to work on what was to be her last considerable achievement in the novel, the historical work published in 1925 under the title *The Big House of Inver*.

As has been noted earlier, Edith and Martin had been excited, during the writing of their first novel, *An Irish Cousin*, by "an ideal of Art" which came to them as a result of a visit they paid to an old kinswoman living out her last days in a decaying mansion. This image of the declining Big House presides over their fictions, both grave and gay. Such houses appear in the "R.M." stories as part of the landscape of the comedy. They are central to *The Real Charlotte* and *Mount Music*. In the spring of 1912, before she went to stay with Lady Gregory at Coole, Martin had been taken to see yet another house of this kind and had once again been deeply moved by the experience. The house in question was Tyrone House in Galway, the seat of an old Galway family, the St. Georges, who had declined from their early grandeur and "gone native," living with village girls, breeding many bastards, fighting and quarreling among themselves, until all their former greatness had disappeared and all that was left was the empty house and a confused memory of much folly. In a letter to Edith, Martin reported her visit to Tyrone House and its powerful effect upon her:

March 18, 1912.

Yesterday I drove to see X-House. A great cut stone house of three stories. . . .

Perfectly empty. . . . It is on a long promontory by the sea, and there rioted three or four generations of X-s, living with country women, occasionally marrying them, all illegitimate four times over. . . . About one hundred and fifty years ago a very grand Lady ———— married the head of the family and lived there, and was so corroded with pride that she would not allow her two daughters to associate with the neighbours of her own class. She lived to see them marry two of the men in the yard. . . .

Yesterday, as we left, an old Miss X, daughter of the last owner, was at the door in a little donkey-trap. She lives near in an old castle, and since her people died she will not go into X-House, or into the enormous yard, or the beautiful old garden.

She was a strange mixture of distinction and commonness, like her breeding, and it was very sad to see her at the door of that great house.

If we dared to write up that subject ————!

Yours ever,
Martin

In *The Big House of Inver* Edith did so dare and, in doing so, achieved her last fictional triumph. This novel, chronicling the ruin of the Prendevilles, is in direct line of descent from Maria Edgeworth's *Castle Rackrent,* that great seminal account of the ruin of a once splendid family. Maria Edgeworth had given her narrative a peculiar power by choosing as her narrator one of the suppressed peasantry, and had achieved in Thady Quirke a terrible portrait of slavery. At the heart of *The Big House of Inver* there is a finely conceived character of equal power, Shibby Pindy, a by-blow of the Prendeville line whose very name itself is, literally, a debasement, a corroded version of "Isabella Prendeville," which indicates her illegitimate status. Edith wrings from Shibby's semi-savage innocence the sort of moral force which Maria Edgeworth derived from Thady Quirke's naive fidelity to his wretched masters. Shibby is determined to restore the Prendeville grandeur by marrying her beloved half-brother, Kit, to a wealthy heiress and to this end she toils with a self-lessness which is the most powerful rebuke to the family's cynical and indifferent roisterings. In her ignorance and innocence, she fills the great rooms of the Big House of Inver with gimcrack rubbish purchased with her heart's blood at local auctions. The Prendevilles have squandered their inheritance with a dreadful combination of bravura and folly and poor Shibby, equipped with nothing but determination and a fierce ideal, labors to repair the damages of many reckless generations. In her battle with heredity she is doomed to failure, but in fighting the battle with a fierce and singleminded love, she transcends the ruin and folly of the past. Unwilling to inflict the stigma of illegitimacy on children of her own, she refuses to marry the local doctor, whom she loves, and bestows all her fierce affection on the wayward Kit. Shibby Pindy, lonely, gallant, warmhearted, lovingly managerial, must have been very close to the impulsive heart of her creator, herself a dominant and lonely figure, now at the last stage of her creative life. Over the whole tale broods the Big House of Inver itself, retaining its grandeur and beauty of proportion into an age unworthy of these qualities and finally destroyed by the last of the playboy Prendevilles, decrepit old Captain Jas.

Like *Mount Music,* this novel is big in conception and contains in Shibby and Old Johnny Weldon characters on the grand scale. Edith occasionally indulges in regrettably coy parentheses, to underline some heavy or obvious jest in passing, and she is inclined, also, to her old lapse of explaining character in terms of class. In general, however, the story survives the occasional blemishes in the narration and drives energetically on to its inevitable conclusion. The writer's absorption in her theme triumphs over aesthetic deficiencies which tended to dominate her more flaccid fictions. This was to be her last, considerable, fictional achievement.

Written in Edith's seventieth year, *French Leave* (1928) is a light and pleasantly nostalgic novel which makes use of the author's memories of her Drishane childhood and of her student days in Paris at the ateliers of Colarossi and Délécluse. The heroine, Patricia Kirwan, is a lively version of Edith's vision of herself.

Energetic, scornful of older sisters who are content to marry and settle down, and eager for adventure, Patsy also longs for the larger life of Europe. She plays the organ in the local church (as Edith herself did for an amazing seventy-five years) , paints, adores dogs and yearns for freedom. She captivates two men, one of them socially acceptable and the other a social inferior. Lord Jimmy Corran is an eligible young peer and a distant connection of Patsy's family. George Lester is the talented artist son of an aggressively Protestant farmer. Patsy and George are thrown together when they both escape to the studios of Paris, after rows with their respective fathers. Jimmy Corran has been on the point of declaring his love for Patsy before she leaves Ireland but settles for financing her trip instead. Once Patsy is safely arrived in Paris, Edith has an opportunity to describe the sort of life she had lived herself as an art student in Paris in her twenties and the story moves undemandingly along on this level, with Patsy briefly attracted to George Lester but finally settling for a return to Ireland, home and duty in the form of an inevitable marriage with young Lord Corran.

Edith's last novel, *Sarah's Youth* (1938), appeared ten years later. In it, the octogenarian author trots forth with a good deal of brio all the hobby-horses on which her weaker fictions depend. Sarah Heritage-Dixon is the tomboy heroine who careers through the book from tantrum to tantrum, from prank to prank. She falls in love with young Tim Kavanagh, son of the local smith, who is a marvel with horses and dogs and is destined to be a vet. He is, of course, utterly unsuitable as a husband for the better-bred Sarah, and she is compelled to confront this social obviosity in an improbable denouement involving her illegitimate sister. There is also an older cousin who is hopelessly enamored of Sarah and a younger cousin who is introduced as a more likely suitor. Sarah does not, in fact, marry any of them but ends the book by "whipping hounds" for Big Miss Mary, the Amazonian M.F.H. on whom she has a school-girl crush. Edith's two alter-egos, romping school-girl and genial but dominant Master of Fox Hounds, merge into one. Even if the whole thing is on the level of girlish romp rather than serious fiction, it is still an engagingly energetic performance for its elderly author.

8

Edith Somerville's Later Years and an Appraisal of the Writers' Achievement

Edith Somerville was to live to a great age, surviving almost a quarter of a century after the publication of *The Big House of Inver* and right through the difficult years of the second World War. Thus, her life, begun in the heyday of Victoria's reign, was to outlast the final remnants of the British Imperial glory which her class had taken so much for granted. It was not merely that she survived into a radically altered Ireland; she lived long enough to see a changed universe. Appropriately enough for a woman of her courageous spirit, her last quarter of a century saw her emerge more into the public eye and take her place there as a celebrated woman of letters. Her long friendship with the well-known musician and composer, Ethel Smyth, was instrumental in making her better known to the public.

The two women, both variously talented, both highly individualistic and energetic, met for the first time in 1919 at the home of Lady Kenmare and began an intense friendship. An immediate result of their first encounter was the exhibition of Edith's paintings at the Goupil Gallery in London in the following year, an exhibition which netted Edith £400 from a public that was delighted to pay well for the paintings of a writer in whose literary efforts it had for so long been taking pleasure. Ethel Smyth wrote an enthusiastic prefatory note for the catalogue and predicted, accurately as it transpired, that the public would "recognize landscapes they have long since known in another medium." The profits of the exhibition, added to some royalties from Ethel Smyth's own work, *Impressions that Remained,* helped to finance the trip the two made together to Sicily in 1920.

A keen traveller since her early days, Edith went to Spain in 1926. Accounts of both the Sicilian and Spanish trips are included in *Happy Days* (1946). Another London exhibition, at Walker's Gallery in 1927, proved less financially successful than the earlier one at the Goupil Gallery but, while she was in London this time, Edith again enjoyed herself greatly, lunching and dining out frequently and generally meeting with acclaim from London society. The year 1928 was saddened for her by the death of her brother Aylmer, founder of the West Carbery Hunt which had provided her with some of her greatest pleasures and with unfailing material for her writing.

Early the following year, in February 1929, when she

was already over seventy, she set out with her sister Hildegarde, Lady Coghill, on her most ambitious trip of all, to the United States. She had been invited to go on a lecture tour and she needed the money which such a tour promised to provide. An account of her American trip is to be found in the book which resulted from it, *The States through Irish Eyes* (1930). New York, South Carolina, Boston, New Haven and Philadelphia were among the places visited and Edith and her younger sister were entertained lavishly everywhere. For the first time, Edith was really lionized and she revelled in her new-found fame. An exhibition of her paintings was held in the Ackermann Galleries in New York and she made £1500 by it, far more than she had ever previously got from any exhibition of her work. The American tour lasted nearly three months and Edith was back in Drishane in mid-May, delighted with the success, both financial and personal, of her first transatlantic venture.

In the following year, she made a trip to Paris and revisited her old art school there. She found the studios "as old and rickety as ever, untouched by modernity," but the young students of 1930, with their modernistic work, made her feel "like Rip van Winkle, or even his ghost" and, after working briefly from the model with the students at Colarossi's, she went on to what had been the studio of Délécluse and found that, there too, times and art fashions had changed too much for her. An account of this rather daunting trip into the past is included in Ch. VI of *Happy Days* (1946).

Her next literary project was a work of family piety,

a biography of the much-revered ancestor whom Edith shared with Martin, Charles Kendal Bushe, a celebrated Lord Chief Justice of Ireland in the early nineteenth century. Characteristically, Edith went about her task in a highly individualistic manner. She had done a certain amount of conventional research on her subject in the British Museum during 1930 but supplemented this by taking the unusual step of calling up her subject from the dead in several seances. The book, *An Incorruptible Irishman,* appeared in 1932.

In this year also, Edith began to meet with a good deal of public recognition in her own country. Trinity College, Dublin delighted her by conferring upon her the degree of Doctor of Letters, an honor in which she asked that Martin's name be coupled with her own, and, later in the same year, W. B. Yeats invited her to become a member of the newly founded Irish Academy of Letters. She went to Dublin in 1933 to attend a dinner given by the Academy and sat between Yeats and George Russell and met many prominent Irish artists. Nine years later, the Academy bestowed on her the Gregory Gold Medal, its most important literary award.

In spite of all the public acclaim, however, these were years in which Edith was driven to selling some of her manuscripts to make money to pay the home farm's debts. She also traded in horses, buying them locally in County Cork and selling them to American purchasers. In 1935, she collaborated with Geraldine Cummins (subsequently her first biographer) in a film scenario of *An Irish Cousin* but nothing came of the attempt to place the scenario. In 1936, Edith and the whole Somerville connection were dealt a shattering blow by the murder of her brother Boyle. Boyle Somerville, five years younger than Edith, was a retired Admiral, a scholarly and able man who had published dictionaries of languages in New Hebrides, New Georgia, and the Solomon Islands and written papers for various anthropological and antiquarian journals. He was living in retirement with his wife, Mab, at the Point House in Castle Townshend. On an evening in late March, 1936, he was gunned down at his own frontdoor by unidentified assailants. The whole of Ireland was outraged and Eamon de Valera, then head of the Irish government, expressed his horror at the murder. The shocking incident was never fully explained nor were the assailants ever identified. Boyle had been working on a book on Will Mariner, a contemporary of Captain Cook. Edith took it upon herself to revise the Ms. and the book was subsequently published by Faber. She also published, in 1940, the *Records of the Somerville Family of Castlehaven and Drishane from 1174 to 1940*, joining her name with Boyle's, as co-authors, on the title-page of the work.

During the thirties, in addition to *Sarah's Youth,* Edith also published two collections of essays, *The Smile and the Tear* (1933) and *The Sweet Cry of Hounds* (1936), and, ever indefatigable, set out for America once more in 1936. This trip was a business one during which she hoped to familiarize herself with the American horse market for purposes of future trading. Shortly after her arrival in America, however, she was taken ill with an attack of phlebitis and had to cut short her trip and return home. During the war years which soon followed, Edith lived on at Drishane House with her younger sister, Hildegarde, and her brother Cameron. Times were far from easy and Edith was now over eighty. In 1942, Cameron died and left Drishane to his nephew Desmond who was overseas with the British army. It was arranged that Edith and Hildegarde would continue to live at Drishane for the time being, an arrangement made possible by the generosity of her younger brother, Jack Somerville. During the war years, the ageing Edith produced another book of reminiscent essays, *Notions in Garrison* (1941) and when the war had ended and she was drawing close to her ninetieth year she published yet another collection of "essays of sorts" under the title *Happy Days* (1946). Her last published work appeared in the very year of her death. It was *Maria and Some Other Dogs* (1949).

Late in 1946, Edith left Drishane House of which she had been mistress for over half a century, and moved with her sister, Hildegarde, into a house, in the main street of Castle Townshend, which bore the euphoric title of "Tally-Ho." Here, the ageing author spent her last years, growing gradually feebler, crippled by rheumatism and further incapacitated by a severe fall which she sustained in May 1947. Game to the last, however, she kept up her correspondence and her diaries almost to the end. Appropriately enough, Edith's first biographer, Geraldine Cummins, gave the chapter in which she describes these last years the title, "Still at Work." Edith Somerville died at "Tally-Ho" on 8 October 1949 and was buried beside her beloved cousin and collaborator, under the eastern wall of St. Barrahane's church, three days later. At her own request, a striking-looking uncarved boulder marks her grave. Its distinctiveness, its difference from more conventional headstones, seems to highlight in a final fashion her life-long preference for the informal, her joy in what she called "the personal element" in human affairs.

Summary of a literary career is never a simple matter. Even with the greatest there are things we would wish otherwise. The task is made yet more difficult when, as is the case with Somerville and Ross, we treat of a closely knit partnership, one member of which outlived the other by a whole generation. The knitting together of the two lives seems to increase in geometric rather than arithmetic progression the haps and accidents which control literary lives and the sundering of the partnership, instead of simplifying issues, creates new ones.

Cutting boldly through all the reservations which threaten to inhibit the formation of any conclusion, one would wish, first of all, to claim for these writers that they are great givers of pleasure, great entertainers. Edith reports of Violet that an old countrywoman said of her: "Sure ye're always laughing! That ye may laugh in the sight of the Glory of Heaven!" The old woman went to the heart of the matter. Preeminently, it is the "R.M." stories one thinks of in this connection, but many of the essays and articles, as well as the novels, contrive to amuse us with great good-humor. The writers' comic confidence is solidly based on their security within their social group, and, paradoxically, their interpretation of the tragedy of their class can be traced to the same source. Better than anyone else they knew the grave and the gay sides of their worlds. *The Real Charlotte* is, of course, their greatest achievement in any mode but it should not be forgotten that, after Martin's death, Edith carried on this branch of their activities very creditably in such novels as *Mount Music* and *The Big House of Inver*. Had Violet lived, as Edith did, to see the emergence of modern Ireland, perhaps they might together have provided in another great novel the sort of searching commentary on the new Ireland which they had already achieved about the old. This complex partnership, so tragically sundered in mid-stream, bristles with conjecture. If Martin had lived; if the need for money had not been so keen; if Martin's ill-health had not interfered, and so on and so on.

A truce to such pointless speculation! The achievement, after all, is solid enough. It includes what is, arguably, the finest Irish novel of the nineteenth century and a set of the funniest stories ever written. Somerville and Ross may not always function at their highest voltage, but when they do, their brilliance is undeniable.

Socially secure in a poor country, socially insecure in a declining class, they looked at their Irish world with clarity, geniality and much sympathetic insight. We should be grateful for what they did, not captious about what they did not do. In an Ireland which has recently seen the emergence of old animosities which many had thought dead and buried, the lives and works of these two talented women and their special, high-spirited geniality have once again acquired a genuine relevance.

Tabular Chronology

1858 Edith Oenone Somerville born at Corfu, 2nd May.

1862 Violet Florence Martin born at Ross House, Co. Galway, 11th June.

1872 Robert Martin closes Ross House on father's death.

Violet and mother move to Dublin.

1884 Edith studies art at Düsseldorf and Paris.

1886 Cousins meet for first time at Castle Townshend.

1887 They visit London and Paris.

1888 Mrs Martin and Violet re-open Ross House.

1889 First novel, *An Irish Cousin*, published by Richard Bentley & Son.

1890 Edith and Martin tour Connemara for *Lady's Pictorial*.

1891 *Naboth's Vineyard*. Tour of French vineyards.

1892 *Through Connemara in a Governess Cart*.

1893 *In the Vine Country*. Tours in Wales (June) and Denmark (September). Visit to Oxford.

1894 *The Real Charlotte:* They visit Paris. Edith studies at art school again.

1895 Martin visits Scotland, meets Andrew Lang at St. Andrews.

Both visit Aran Islands (May–June) and do election work in East Anglia later.

Beggars on Horseback.

Edith's mother dies. Edith becomes mistress of Drishane House.

1896 J. B. Pinker becomes their literary agent.

1897 *The Silver Fox.*

1898 Edith's father dies.

"R.M." stories begun during visit to Étaples.

Martin badly injured by fall from horse (November).

1899 *Some Experiences of an Irish R.M.*

Both in Paris for four months.

1900 Martin visits Buxton for health reasons.

1901 Martin meets W. B. Yeats at Lady Gregory's house, Coole.

1902 *A Patrick's Day Hunt.*

J.B. Pinker visits Drishane. Urges them to write more "R.M." stories.

1903 Edith becomes M.F.H. of West Carbery Fox Hounds.

All on the Irish Shore

Slipper's ABC of Fox Hunting

1904 Edith and Martin visit Amélie-les-Bains.

1905 Martin attends several performances at Abbey Theatre.

Death of Martin's brother, Robert.

1906 Death of Martin's mother.

Some Irish Yesterdays.

1908 *Further Experiences of an Irish R.M.*
     Edith resigns as M.F.H.
1910 Edith and Martin attend banquet for Irish women
     writers given by Corinthian Dinner Committee
     in Dublin.
     They visit Pinker at his home in Surrey.
1911 *Dan Russel the Fox.*
1912 Edith reestablishes the West Carbery Fox-Hounds
     (M.F.H. 1912–19).
1913 Edith President of Munster Women's Franchise
     League; Martin a Vice-President.
1915 *In Mr Knox's Country.*
     Cousins holiday together in Kerry.
     Death of Violet Florence Martin in Cork, 21 De-
     cember. Funeral at Castle Townshend.
1916 Edith visits England for health reasons, stays with
     her brother, Cameron.
     Signs petition for clemency for leaders of Easter
     Rising.
     Engages in automatic writing with friend, Jem
     Barlow, and believes she has made contact with
     Martin's spirit. Encouraged to write again.
1917 *Irish Memories.*
1919 Edith stays at home of Sir Horace Plunkett, in
     Dublin and meets George Russell ("A.E.").
     Meets Ethel Smyth at Lady Kenmare's house and
     begins long, intense friendship. Ethel Smyth
     visits Drishane House and offers to arrange
     London exhibition of Edith's paintings. Edith
     visits Ethel's home in December.
     Mount Music.

1920 Exhibition of paintings at Goupil Gallery, London.

Trip to Sicily with Ethel Smyth.

Ethel Smyth visits Drishane House, while Edith is ill.

Edith visits baths at Dax in South of France and visits Ethel Smyth's home, on return.

Strayaways.

1921 *An Enthusiast.*

1923 Edith visits Ethel Smyth.

Longmans give advance of £400 on *Wheel-Tracks.*

Successful exhibition of paintings at Walkers, Bond Street.

1925 *The Big House of Inver.*

1926 Edith stays with Ethel Smyth's sister in London and meets George Moore.

Trip to Spain.

1927 Edith attends mass meeting of spiritualists at Albert Hall.

Another, less successful, exhibition at Walker's Gallery.

Friendship with spiritualist Geraldine Cummins begins.

1928 Death of Edith's brother, Aylmer.

French Leave.

1929 Successful lecture-tour in U.S.A. (Feb.–May). Exhibition of paintings at Ackermann Galleries, New York, makes £1500.

Work begun on comedy, *A Horse! A Horse!,* based on "R.M." stories.

1930 *The States Through Irish Eyes.*

Edith visits her old art-schools in Paris.

Visit to Ethel Smyth.

Works at British Museum in preparation for biography of Charles Kendal Bushe.

1932 *An Incorruptible Irishman.*

Trinity College, Dublin awards Edith a D.Litt.

W. B. Yeats invites her to join Irish Academy of Letters.

Geraldine Cummins fails to interest theatrical friend in *A Horse! A Horse!*

1933 Edith attends Irish Academy of Letters dinner at Jammet's restaurant, Dublin and meets many Irish writers and artists.

The Smile and the Tear.

1934 Edith raises £1250 by sale of Mss. (purchased by the Comte de Suzannet). Also exports horses to America.

1935 Geraldine Cummins collaborates with Edith on film scenario of *An Irish Cousin.*

1936 Murder of Edith's brother, Admiral Boyle Somerville.

The Sweet Cry of Hounds.

Edith exports horses to America in partnership with American friend, Sylvia Warren. Makes short business trip to America but forced, by illness, to return.

1938 *Sarah's Youth.*

Exhibition of paintings in New York.

1940 *Somerville Family Records.*

1941 *Notions in Garrison.*

Edith stays at home of American Ambassador in Dublin (David Gray).

Meets president of Irish Free State, Dr Douglas Hyde.

Edith awarded Gregory Medal by Irish Academy of Letters.

1942 Death of Edith's favourite brother, Cameron. Drishane House passes to her nephew, Desmond Somerville.

1944 Death of Dame Ethel Smyth.

1945 Edith guest of honour at Swift bi-centenary banquet in Cork.

1946 *Happy Days.*

Sale of some Somerville and Ross Mss. at Sotheby's.

Edith writes essay "Two of a Trade" for first issue of *Irish Writing* (her last contribution to a periodical).

She leaves Drishane House and moves with her sister, Hildegarde, into "Tally-Ho."

1947 Jem Barlow, Edith's clairvoyant friend, dies.

Edith injured in fall.

1948 She makes her will.

Her nephew, Professor Nevill Coghill, broadcasts talk about her for the B.B.C. on her ninetieth birthday.

Oxford University Press includes *The Real Charlotte* in its "World's Classics" series.

1949 *Maria and Some Other Dogs.*

Death of Edith Oenone Somerville at Castle Townshend, 8th October.

Selected Bibliography

(A) PRINCIPAL WORKS:

An Irish Cousin. London: Richard Bentley & Son, 1889.

Naboth's Vineyard. London: Spencer Blackett, 1891.

Through Connemara in a Governess Cart. London: W. H. Allen & Co. Ltd., 1892.

In The Vine Country. London: W. H. Allen & Co. Ltd., 1893.

The Real Charlotte. London: Ward and Downey Ltd., 1894.

Beggars on Horseback. Edinburgh and London: William Blackwood & Sons, 1895.

The Silver Fox. London: Lawrence & Bullen Ltd., 1898.

Some Experiences of An Irish R.M. London: Longmans, Green & Co., 1899.

A Patrick's Day Hunt. London: Archibald Constable & Co. Ltd., 1902.

All On the Irish Shore. London: Longmans, Green & Co., 1903.

Slipper's ABC of Fox Hunting. London: Longmans, Green & Co., 1903.

Some Irish Yesterdays. London: Longmans, Green & Co., 1906.

Further Experiences of An Irish R.M. London: Longmans, Green & Co., 1908.

Dan Russel the Fox. London: Methuen & Co. Ltd., 1911.

In Mr Knox's Country. London: Longmans, Green & Co., 1915.

Irish Memories. London: Longmans, Green & Co., 1917.

Mount Music. London: Longmans, Green & Co., 1919.

Stray-Aways. London: Longmans, Green & Co., 1920.

An Enthusiast. London: Longmans, Green & Co., 1921.

Wheel-Tracks. London: Longmans, Green & Co., 1923.

The Big House of Inver. London: William Heinemann Ltd., 1925.

French Leave. London: William Heinemann Ltd., 1928.

The States Through Irish Eyes. Boston & New York: Houghton Mifflin Co., 1930 (1st English ed. London, William Heinemann Ltd., 1931.)

An Incorruptible Irishman. London: Ivor Nicholson & Watson, 1932.

The Smile And The Tear. London: Methuen & Co. Ltd., 1933.

The Sweet Cry of Hounds. London: Methuen & Co. Ltd., 1936.

Sarah's Youth. London: Longmans, Green & Co., 1938.

Notions in Garrison. London: Methuen & Co. Ltd., 1941.

Happy Days. London: Longmans, Green & Co., 1946.

Maria and Some Other Dogs. London: Methuen & Co. Ltd., 1949.

(B) STANDARD BIBLIOGRAPHIES:

i. ed. Hudson, Elizabeth (explanatory notes by Edith Somerville). *A Bibliography of the First Editions of the Works of E. Œ. Somerville and Martin Ross.* New York: The Sporting Gallery and Bookshop Inc., 1942.

ii. Sadleir, Michael, *XIX Century Fiction.* Cambridge University Press, 1951, Vol. 1, pp. 329–331.

iii. ed. Vaughan, Robert. *The First Editions of Edith Oenone Somerville and Violet Florence Martin.*

Inc. in Cummins, Geraldine. *Dr. E. Œ. Somerville: A Biography*. London: Andrew Dakers Ltd., 1952, pp. 243–271.

(C) BIOGRAPHIES:

Collis, Maurice. *Somerville and Ross: A Biography*. London: Faber and Faber, 1968.
Cummins, Geraldine. *Dr. E. Œ Somerville: A Biography*. London: Andrew Dakers Ltd., 1952.

(D) CRITICAL STUDIES:

Fehlmann, Guy. *Somerville et Ross: témoins de l'Irlande d'hier*. Caen: Faculté des Lettres et Sciences Humaine de l'Université de Caen, 1970.
Powell, Violet. *The Irish Cousins*. London: Heinemann, 1970.

(E) A SELECTION OF CRITICAL ARTICLES:

Coghill, Sir Patrick. "Somerville and Ross." *Hermathena*, No. 79 (1952), pp. 47–60.
Cronin, John. "Dominant Themes in the Novels of Somerville and Ross." *Somerville and Ross: A Symposium*. Belfast: Institute of Irish Studies, Queen's University, 1968, pp. 8–18.
Flanagan, Thomas. "The Big House of Ross-Drishane." *The Kenyon Review*, Vol. 28, No. 1 (Jan. 1966), pp. 54–78.
Graves, C. L. "The Lighter Side of Irish Life." *Quarterly Review*, Vol. 219, No. 436 (July 1913), pp. 26–47.
———. "Martin Ross." *National Review* (May 1918).
Gwynn, Stephen. "The Secret of Ireland." *Macmillan's Magazine*, 83 (1900–1901), pp. 410–419.
———. "Lever's Successors." *Edinburgh Review*, July 1913.

Lowell, Amy. "To Two Unknown Ladies." *North American Review* (June 1919) , p. 263.

MacCarthy, B. G. "E. Œ. Somerville and Martin Ross." *Studies,* Vol. 24 (1945) , pp. 183–194.

McMahon, Sean. "John Bull's Other Island: A Consideration of *The Real Charlotte* by Somerville and Ross." *Eire-Ireland,* Vol. 3, No. 4 (Winter 1968) , pp. 119–135.

Mitchell, Hilary. "Somerville and Ross: Amateur to Professional." *Somerville and Ross: A Symposium,* Belfast: Institute of Irish Studies, Queen's University, 1968, pp. 20–37.

O'Brien, Conor Cruise. "Somerville and Ross" (radio talk) . *Writers and Politics,* London: Chatto and Windus, 1965.

Power, Ann. "The Big House of Somerville and Ross." *The Dubliner* (Spring 1964) , pp. 43–53.

Pritchett, V. S. "The Irish R.M." *The Living Novel and Later Appreciations,* New York: Vintage Books, 1947, pp. 199–205.

Quiller-Couch, Sir Arthur. "Tribute to Ireland." *The Poet as Citizen and Other Papers,* Cambridge University Press, 1934, pp. 218–226.

Trotter, Elizabeth Stanley. "Humour With a Gender." *Atlantic Monthly,* Vol. 130, No. 6 (December 1922) .

Watson, Cresap S. "The Somerville and Ross Tour Journals." *Dublin Magazine* (July–Sept. 1953) , pp. 26–31.

Williams, Orlo. "A Little Classic of the Future." *London Mercury,* Vol. 1, No. 5 (March 1920) , pp. 555–564.

———. *Some Great English Novels (Studies in the Art of Fiction).* London: Methuen & Co. Ltd., 1926.